RECIPES FROM THE HEARTLAND

Recipes from the Heartland

The Country Women's Institutes
of New Zealand
COOKBOOK

VIKING

Penguin Books (NZ) Ltd, 182-190 Wairau Road, Auckland 10, New Zealand
Penguin Books Ltd, 27 Wrights Lane, London W8 5TZ, England
Penguin USA, 375 Hudson Street, New York, NY 10014, United States
Penguin Books Australia Ltd, 487 Maroondah Highway, Ringwood, Australia 3134
Penguin Books Canada Ltd, 10 Alcorn Avenue, Toronto, Canada M4V 3B2

Penguin Books Ltd, Registered Offices: Harmondsworth, Middlesex, England

First published by Penguin Books New Zealand, 1995

10 9 8 7 6 5 4 3 2

Text © NZ Federation of Country Women's Institutes 1995

Designed and produced by Stephen Barnett
Typeset by Jazz Graphics, Auckland
Printed by Condor Production Co. Ltd, Hong Kong

ISBN 0-670-86472-2

Front cover photograph ©TRANZ.
Back cover photographs courtesy Rotorua Museum and Andris Apse.

The recipes in this book are the creation of members of the New Zealand Federation of
Country Women's Institutes. Any similarity to existing recipes is coincidental. Every care
has been taken to ensure that the contents of this work are accurate. However the producer
and publisher do not accept responsibility for the consequences if any errors or omissions
have occurred.

CONTENTS

MEASUREMENTS

Metric Kitchen Measures

15ml	= 1 tablespoon	1.25ml	= ¼ teaspoon
10ml	= 1 dessertspoon	2 teaspoons	= 1 dessertspoon
5ml	= 1 teaspoon	3 teaspoons	= 1 tablespoon
2.5ml	= ½ teaspoon		

Cups

1000ml	= 1 litre	= 4 cups	62.5ml	= ¼ cup
500ml	= ½ litre	= 2 cup	1 cup (approx)	= 16 tablespoons
250ml	= ¼ litre	= 1 cup	1 litre	= 4 cups
125ml	= ½ cup			

Weights and Measures
Butter and Sugar

500g or 0.5 kilogram (kg)	= 2 cups
15g	= 1 tablespoon
10g	= 1 dessertspoon

Flour

½ kg	= 4 cups (sifted)
15g	= 2 tablespoon
10g	= 2 dessertspoons

OVEN TEMPERATURES – degrees Celsius (°C)

below 140	Cool
140–160	Slow
160–180	Moderately slow
180–190	Moderate
190–200	Moderately hot
200–220	Hot
230–240	Very hot

Recipe ingredients mainly use standard cups and spoons and you may require a good set of kitchen scales. Measures should be taken level.

Foreword

IN A PREFACE to the first edition of *The Cookery Book of the New Zealand Women's Institutes* published in 1934, the then Dominion president, M. Paterson, noted that the cookbook marked a stage in the evolution of the Institutes' notion that 'if you know a good thing, pass it on'.

All across the country, individual institutes had over the years held competitions for the 'best plate of scones, the best cake and even the best dinner'. After that, 'it seemed a natural thing to invite members to send in their recipes for publication in book form'. The result was a first collection of recipes in *The Cookery Book*. Numerous revised and updated editions have followed through the years.

This new edition, *Recipes from the Heartland,* continues the line. Like its predecessors, it presents a wonderful collection of tried and true recipes whose origins are the kitchens of CWI members.

The first *Cookery Book* also carried a foreword by Ann Elizabeth Jerome Spencer, the founder of CWI in New Zealand:

> A foreword to a cookery book may well suggest to the reader the analogy of grace before meat, thoughts of gratitude for the good things to follow, for the better methods and ways that invention and science have brought to us through labour's airy devices and knowledge of food values. Thus, no one seeking in the following pages will encounter the kind of recipe that began, 'Take pigs; hew them into gobbets'. Nor will the hospitable hostess of the present day be planning the kind of 'humble Feast' recorded by Gervase Markham as being an ordinary proportion which any good man may keep in his family for the entertainment of his true and worthy friends. 'Sixteen dishes were a good proportion for one course unto one messe' and these included 'A shield of brawn with mustard, a chine of beef rosted, a neat'o tongue rosted, chewets baked, a goose

rosted, a swan rosted, an Olive-pye, and custard or dousets.' Many other causes for thankfulness may suggest themselves and, whatever they be, doubtless a thankful heart inspiring skilful hands can impart a subtly improved savour to any dish.

Or, regarded from another aspect, perhaps a foreword should play the part of an aperrtif, and whet the appetite for trying the excellent and improved recipes that follow in these pages. To this end we need but inform you fair readers, that herein is a choice selection of those good things known to Women's Institute members which they rejoice to have this opportunity of passing on to you.

Such sentiment is as good today as it was then. Good cooking!

Preface

THIS BOOK is a treasure trove of hundreds of favourite recipes gathered from members of the Country Women's Institutes around New Zealand. Many will have been passed on from generation to generation and we are indebted to all members who have so generously shared these recipes with us.

Country Women's Institutes has its origins in the Women's Institute founded in Canada in 1897, in the small country centre of Stoney Creek, Ontario. In 1915, following the success and spread of the organisation in Canada, the first Institute in Great Britain was started. From there the idea was introduced to New Zealand by Miss Ann Elizabeth Jerome Spencer on her return from war work in England. Early in February 1921 the first Women's Institute was founded at Rissington in northern Hawkes Bay.

Country Women's Institutes developed remarkably in the intervening years. Our motto 'For Home and Country' still applies in the very different world of the 1990s as Institutes in towns as well as in rural areas seek to develop and to work for the benefit of the community and the nation. Begun as an organisation to break down the physical isolation of women in the country, today CWI also answers the needs of city women who can be just as isolated. The organisation offers a voice for women locally and nationally; friendship, support, and a sharing of the vast knowledge of the many skills members have – handcraft, homecraft, choral, drama, horticulture and public speaking.

In March 1950 the Institute purchased a suitable building in Wellington for its National Headquarters, and 1984 saw the opening of a refurbished Jerome Spencer House – named after our founder. The extensive improvements and extensions to the original building were made possible by the generosity and enthusiasm of Country Women's Institutes members.

The
Cookery Book
of the
N.Z. Women's Institute

Containing

Over 900 Tested Recipes

And many useful hints.

———

Price 1/6

Postage 3d extra.

———

1934.

Printed by Kerslake and Billens, Ltd., Printers, Levin.

An organisation is known by its accomplishments. It would be impossible to enumerate all that CWI has achieved in New Zealand and overseas since 1921. Members' efforts have ranged from work to help the national war efforts in the 1940s – such as making camouflage nets, sending fat to Britain, home nursing and making up soldiers' parcels – to a special project in the late 1980s that saw CWI working with school children throughout New Zealand to knit peggy square rugs for use by refugees in Uganda. In all, 4200 woollen cot blankets were shipped to Uganda to be presented to the children of that country. More recently, Operation Health Camp gave CWI members the opportunity to be actively involved in assisting with practical and financial support to New Zealand's camps.

Internationally, members have been most generous in their support of the South Pacific Literary Project which, in conjunction with the Save the Children (New Zealand) Fund, aims to increase the rate of literacy of women in remote villages in Papua New Guinea.

To mark the Golden Jubilee of CWI, members raised money to purchase a punch-index machine for use in testing newborn babies for metabolic disorders. The reponse was so great that surplus funds were able to be invested and the interest used for a medical research scholarship. Some areas of this research include the improved care of babies with cancer, research into blindness associated with diabetes, cystic fibrosis, and asthma research.

Through the Country Women's Institutes so many lives have been enriched with knowledge, friendship and practical support, with members always so willing to share their expertise and skills with others. Whether you are an experienced cook or a beginner, our members hope that this book, a comprehensive collection of recipes for all occasions, will give you success and pleasure in your cooking.

AVELDA HOWIE
National President
1995

Appetisers and Entrées

APPETISERS AND ENTRÉES

Appetisers

♦ COCKTAIL SNACKS

Base:
Medium-sliced square white bread. Either cut into 4 rounds with a 4-cm crinkle cutter or cut into 4 squares with crusts trimmed off. Fry in shortening or oil. Bread must be turned quickly when first put into fat to make sure well coated. Drain well. Bread bases can be toasted instead of fried.

Toppings:
Many need to be anchored with a little mayonnaise, made as follows.

Mayonnaise:
1 can sweetened condensed milk, $^3/_4$ can vinegar and $^1/_2$ can water, mixed together.

Following is a variety of toppings that can be used:
♦ Slice of egg, mayonnaise, coloured cocktail onion
♦ Creamed corn, wedge tomato, parsley
♦ 1 x 210g can salmon (cooked with $^1/_4$ bottle cream, small grated onion until thick), cocktail onion and parsley
♦ Cream cheese, grated onion (ham or crushed pineapple) mixed together, topped with small piece pineapple and paprika
♦ Sliced cucumber, sieved cream cheese and parsley
♦ 1 x 2-cm slice banana covered with mayonnaise, sprinkled with chopped walnuts.

♦ OYSTER or CRAYFISH COCKTAIL

3 tbsp slightly whipped cream
1$^1/_2$ tbsp tomato sauce
1 tbsp Worcester sauce
2 drops tabasco sauce
6 oysters per person (or crayfish)
salt and pepper

Put cream in basin and gradually add other sauces and pepper and salt. Add oysters or crayfish and divide into small glasses. Serve very cold with slice of lemon on each glass and brown bread and butter.

♦ SHRIMP COCKTAIL

Line cocktail glasses with tiny leaves of heart lettuce and arrange shrimps in centre. Pour cocktail sauce over. Garnish with parsley and lemon slices. Serve chilled.

♦ PARTY CHEESE BALLS

250g cream cheese
250g cheddar cheese, grated
1 tbsp chopped green capsicum
1 tbsp chopped onion
2 tsp Worcester sauce
salt and pepper
2 tsp chopped mixed green herbs
chopped nuts

Combine softened cream cheese and grated cheese, add capsicum, onion, sauce, seasonings and herbs. Mix well. Shape into balls and roll in nuts. Chill to serve.

♦ CHEESE BALL

250g mild cheese
250g tasty cheese
1 small onion
dash of Worcester sauce
dash of tomato sauce
1-2 tsp chopped gherkins
mayonnaise
chopped walnuts

Grate cheeses and onion. Add Worcester sauce, tomato sauce and gherkins. Mix together with mayonnaise, form into a ball and roll in chopped walnuts. Refrigerate. Serve with crackers.

♦ SMOKED SALMON

Place paper-thin slices of smoked salmon on thin slices of brown toast. Garnish with a little cucumber or pickle.

♦ MUSHROOMS AND HAM

Spread small buttered toast with ham or other paste and finely chopped cooked ham. Cover with finely chopped grilled mushrooms. Serve hot.

♦ CHEESE POTATO CHIPS

1 medium packet of potato chips
1/4 cup grated tasty cheese
1/2 tsp curry powder

Spread chips in large shallow pan. Heat in 160°C oven for 3-4 minutes. Sprinkle with cheese and curry powder mixture. Return to oven until melted cheese adheres to chips.

♦ SEAFOOD COCKTAIL

This may be any mixture of fish, for instance a very good seafood cocktail can be made by combining smoked fish and crayfish with seafood cocktail sauce. Serve chilled.

♦ WHITEBAIT COCKTAIL

Use either cooked fresh or canned whitebait. To cook whitebait toss in butter in a frying pan and cook until they have lost all transparency, 3-4 minutes. Sprinkle with salt and pepper, then cool and place a little in each cocktail glass. Pour over cocktail sauce. Serve chilled.

♦ PAWPAW AND BERRY COCKTAIL

Cut the flesh of a pawpaw into tiny cubes and mix with an equal quantity of small pieces of strawberries or other berries. Place in cocktail glasses and sprinkle each with a few drops of lemon juice. Pour over fruit juice. Rockmelon or honeydew melon may replace the pawpaw. Serve chilled.

♦ WATERMELON ANGOSTURA

Shake 3-4 drops of bitters into each cocktail glass and swill around. Add small cubes of watermelon. Sprinkle each with about ½ teaspoon sugar, then pour over any fruit juice and garnish with lemon or a red cherry. Serve chilled.

♦ MOCK SEAFOOD PATÉ

250g smoked fish
250g cream cheese
1 tbsp lemon juice
1 tbsp grated onion

1 tbsp tomato sauce or 3 tbsp
  mayonnaise
¼ tsp Worcester sauce

Drain the canned fish or poach fresh smoked fish, then mince or chop in blender. If using blender, add remaining ingredients and blend again, otherwise place remaining ingredients into a bowl and thoroughly mix in the minced fish. Press into a small container or shape into a cube. Chill well. Serve with crackers or as spread.

♦ MINTED FRUIT COCKTAIL

Combine 2-3 fruits such as oranges, peaches, gooseberries, mandarins, apricots or pears. Mix together and place in cocktail glasses. Combine the syrups of the fruits chosen and flavour with peppermint essence. Top with lemon slices and a red cherry. Serve chilled.

♦ FRUIT BOUQUET

Mix together tiny cubes of pineapple, apricot and orange or grapefruit. Place in cocktail glasses. Stir together some of the juices, add sherry to taste and pour over the fruit. Bitters may first be shaken into the glasses and swilled around. Serve chilled.

♦ SMOKED OYSTER PATÉ

30g butter
2 rashers bacon, chopped
1/2 tsp chopped basil
125g cream cheese
1/2 tsp Worcester sauce

1 tbsp dry sherry
1/2 tsp lemon juice
salt and pepper
1 x 100g can smoked oysters

Heat butter, cook bacon and chopped basil. Put bacon mixture in blender, blend until fine. Add rest of ingredients, blend until fine or well combined. Spoon into serving dish. Refrigerate overnight.

♦ AVOCADO DIP AND WATER BISCUITS

1 firm, ripe avocado
1 small green onion
1 small tomato
1 tbsp cream *or* cottage cheese
salt and pepper

1 tsp tabasco sauce
1 tsp Worcester sauce
lemon juice
coriander to taste
parmesan to taste

Scoop out avocado carefully (if firm enough, dip can be served in skin). Chop onion and tomato, mix with other ingredients, mash, chill and serve with water biscuits.

♦ SCOTCH WATER BISCUITS (recipe handed down 3 generations)

1 cup flour
1 nut-sized piece of butter

pinch of salt
enough milk to make a paste

Mix and knead. Roll out as thinly as possible and prick to prevent blisters. Stamp into rounds. Bake a pale brown at 160°C. Store in a warm place.

♦ CURRY CURLIES

1 x 750g packet pre-rolled pastry
185g butter

2 tsp curry powder
1 x 250g packet potato chips

Cut pastry into 1 cm strips. Brush both sides of strip with combined melted butter and curry powder. Lightly press finely crushed potato chips on both sides, twist to curl. Place on lightly greased oven tray. Bake at 180°C for 8 minutes or until golden brown. Makes 70.

♦ HONEY WALNUTS

³/₄ cup honey
1 tbsp lemon juice
1 tsp soy sauce

250g walnut halves
castor sugar
oil

Combine honey, lemon juice and soy sauce in a bowl. Add walnuts and mix well. Stir occasionally and stand 2 hours. Drain walnuts, toss in sugar, coating well. Fry walnuts in enough hot oil to cover. Cook until golden brown. Remove walnuts and drain well. These are delicious to serve with drinks.

♦ ORIENTAL DIP

1 cup mayonnaise
1 cup cream cheese
1 clove garlic, mashed
½ tsp salt
1 tbsp chopped parsley

1 tbsp chopped chives
2 tbsp finely chopped ginger
1 tbsp soy sauce
¼ cup finely diced celery
milk

Combine mayonnaise and cream cheese. Beat well and add garlic mashed with salt, parsley, chives, ginger, soy sauce and celery. If necessary thin with milk. When celery is not available, use celery salt and add some sliced brazil nuts for crunchiness. Vegetable sticks can be used for dunking with this or Cheese Dip – try carrot, celery or cucumber sticks. Cut vegetables into finger lengths and stand them in iced water in the fridge until crisp. Drain well and serve in colourful mugs or bowls.

♦ CHEESE DIP

225g tasty cheese, grated
½ cup salad dressing *or* cream
1 tbsp sherry (optional)
1 tsp French mustard

1 tbsp tomato relish
tabasco sauce or Worcester sauce
pepper
milk

Beat cheese and salad dressing or cream. Add sherry, french mustard, tomato relish, tabasco or Worcester sauce and a few grains of pepper. If necessary, use milk to thin to dipping consistency.

♦ CANAPÉS

Canapés are small savouries which can be made in an infinite variety of shapes and flavours and provide possibilities for all kinds of bright, attractive decoration. A savoury mixture is spread on a small base and it is finished with a garnish. As a base use either cheese or plain crackers, small pieces of fried bread, or pieces of pastry. They should be rather small, not more than 5 cm across. Squares, rectangles, rounds, ovals, crescents, stars, diamonds or any other shapes may be chosen. If a bread base is used it may be toasted on one side or two, then lightly buttered or spread with desired mixture and then toasted. If the canapé is served as soon as made, the first method may be used. If made ahead of time and served cold, the bread will be crisper if the second method is followed.

Suggested mixtures for canapes:
- Minced cheese, bacon and chopped pickle or onion.
- Cheddar cheese, cream, cayenne, mashed together and topped with a slice of gherkin.
- Mince crayfish and add mayonnaise, salt and pepper with round of cucumber underneath and garnish with parsley, tomato or pimento.
- Thinly slice smoked salmon to suit toasted or fried rounds of bread. Pipe mayonnaise round edge and garnish with hard-boiled egg and finely stuffed olive.

♦ STUFFED PRUNES

Soak large prunes in sherry until soft. Mash soft tasty cheese with a little cream, sugar, and salt and pepper. Fill prunes with mixture and stick a cocktail stick into the end.

♦ STUFFED CELERY

Use the small centre pieces of heart of celery. Do not cut off the tender little leaves. Some of the tender long stalks may be used as well and cut into pieces about 6 cm long. Mash soft tasty cheese with a little cream. Add sugar, salt and pepper to taste. Chopped chives may be added. Fill hollows with mixture and dust with paprika.

♦ SMOTHERED WALNUTS

Mash soft cheese with sugar and cream. Place about 1 teaspoon of this mixture around a shelled walnut and roll in a ball with the palms of the hands. Roll the balls in finely chopped walnuts, parsley or egg white. Other nuts such as hazel or brazil cut into suitable sizes may be used.

♦ FRANKFURTERS IN HOSPITAL

Split frankfurters in halves lengthwise, but not quite through. Place thin strips of prepared cheese in the cuttings. Cut rinds from bacon and wrap round frankfurters. Secure with cocktail stick. Bake at 180°C until cheese is melted but not running and the bacon crisp. Can be cut into small pieces for cocktail parties. Cut them before splitting. Whole they are excellent for buffet suppers.

♦ ANGELS ON HORSEBACK

Cut bacon rashers into pieces, place an oyster on each piece and sprinkle with two drops of lemon juice. Roll up and secure with a cocktail stick. Bake or grill until bacon is cooked through, but do not cook oysters too long or they will become tough.

♦ SAVOURY ECLAIRS

Asparagus filling:
Make white sauce using half asparagus liquid and half milk. Add salt, pepper, lemon juice and chopped asparagus. Fill cases. May be served hot or cold.

Bacon and egg filling:
Chop rashers of bacon into tiny pieces and fry. In a basin beat 2 eggs and add $1/4$ cup milk, salt and pepper. Pour into bacon and cook gently until scrambled. Fill cases. Sweet corn is also a tasty filling.

♦ MUSHROOMS, PRUNES OR DATES IN BACON BLANKETS

Fried mushrooms, stoned prunes or dates rolled in bacon and grilled on cocktail sticks.

♦ FISH CRISPS

Spread thin slices of bread thickly with finely chopped or minced smoked fish and grated cheese. Roll up, brush with melted butter and bake in moderate oven until golden-brown. Cheese and cayenne, anchovy fillets and Worcester sauce or anchovy paste, shrimps and prawns may be used the same way.

♦ PICKLED HORS-D'OEUVRE PLATTER

Choose any small pickled foods such as pickled onions, walnuts, shrimps, prawns, cauliflowerettes, gherkins, olives, etc., and place each on a cocktail stick. Arrange on a flat platter with a little dish of cocktail sauce in the centre.

♦ COLD CRAYFISH SAVOURIES

Mince crayfish flesh and season with salt and pepper and powdered ginger. Melt 2 tbsp butter in a saucepan and add crayfish. Heat through but do not cook. Press into egg cups and put away for several hours in a cool place. Unmould and serve on lettuce leaves. Garnish with tomato and parsley and 1 teaspoon mayonnaise may be poured over each savoury.

♦ COCKTAIL CRISPS

50g butter
½ cup flour
¼ tsp baking powder
50g potato chips, crushed

75g cheese, grated
2 tbsp finely chopped celery
1 egg
salt

Rub butter into flour and baking powder. Add potato chips, cheese and celery and mix with egg to a stiff dough. Roll out very thinly. Cut into fingers. Put on cold, ungreased tray. Sprinkle well with salt. Bake at 200°C for 10 minutes or until golden-brown.

♦ SWEETCORN FILLING FOR VOL-AU-VENTS

1-2 rashers bacon
1 onion, chopped
2 tbsp butter
2 tbsp flour

salt and pepper
1 cup milk
1 x 310g can sweetcorn
1 egg, beaten

Chop bacon and onion and sauté in a little butter. Combine flour, seasoning, milk and add to bacon and onion. Boil, stirring until thick. Add corn and beaten egg and simmer. Cool before filling cases. Can be made into one large open pie.

Entrées
♦ ASPARAGUS VINAIGRETTE

30*ml* cider vinegar
3 tsp olive oil
¼ tsp mustard
¼ tsp lemon peel
15*ml* lemon juice

15*ml* water
pinch of white pepper
24 asparagus spears, cooked or
    canned
¼ capsicum, thinly sliced

In a jar with a tight fitting lid combine all ingredients except vegetables. Shake well. In a shallow dish arrange asparagus spears, add dressing and gently turn spears in dressing to coat. Scatter sliced capsicum over all. Serves 4.

♦ HERBY MUSHROOMS

225g button mushrooms
2 tbsp oil
1 tsp ground coriander seeds
mixed herbs

parsley
oregano
2 tbsp lemon juice
2 bay leaves

Wash mushrooms, trim stalks and cut into thick slices. Heat oil, add all seasonings then add mushrooms. Cook slowly for about 5 minutes. Serve hot or cold.

♦ BASIC CRÊPES FOR ENTRÉES

In a blender or whizz combine:

1 cup milk	$^3/_4$ cup plain flour
2 large eggs	$^1/_2$ tsp salt

Let stand 15-20 mintues before cooking like pancakes. This makes enough for 16 crêpes.

Now choose the filling you like.

Seafood:

4 tsp margarine	30*ml* lemon juice
$^1/_4$ cup finely chopped celery	4 tsp dry sherry
$^1/_4$ cup finely chopped shallots or onion	pepper
2 cups seafood (shrimps, salmon, crab, smoked fish)	

In a pan heat margarine over medium heat until bubbly. Add celery, shallots or onions and sauté until soft. Add 2 cups mixed seafood – your choice. Add lemon juice, sherry and pepper, and stir until heated. Let cool then fill crêpes. Top with cheese or bechamel sauce. Heat gently and serve.

Chicken-Mushroom:

4 tsp margarine	2 chicken stock cubes
$^1/_2$ cup diced onion	360g cooked, diced chicken
1 cup sliced mushrooms	$^1/_4$ tsp pepper
3 tbsp flour	cooked peas (optional)
$1^1/_2$ cups water	

Heat margarine in pan until bubbly, add onion and sauté until soft. Add mushrooms and sauté another 3 minutes. Add flour and cook stirring constantly for 3 minutes. Remove from heat and gradually add water in which chicken stock has been dissolved. Return to heat and bring to boil. Reduce heat and let simmer 5 minutes. Add chicken, pepper and peas. Cook another 3 minutes then cool before filling crêpes. Put in shallow dish and heat gently. Serve garnished with chopped parsley.

♦ MEAT PANCAKES

$^1/_2$ cup plain flour	250g cooked lamb, diced
$^1/_2$ cup self-raising flour	1 medium onion, finely chopped
1 egg	oil for frying
$1^1/_4$ cups milk	parsley sprigs to garnish
salt and pepper	

Sift the flours into a bowl, make a well in the centre and add the egg. Add the milk a little at a time, beating thoroughly between each addition. Season well with salt and pepper, stir in meat and onion. Grease frying pan with oil, place over moderate heat and cook as for pancakes. Garnish with parsley sprigs. Makes 6-8 pancakes.

Baking and Confectionery

BAKING AND CONFECTIONERY

Cakes
♦ FEIJOA CAKE

100g butter
¾ cup sugar
5 feijoas
1 tsp vanilla
1 egg, beaten

1¾ cups flour
1½ tsp baking powder
1 tsp baking soda
2 tbsp milk

Beat butter and sugar to a cream. Spoon out feijoa flesh and mash with vanilla. Add to creamed butter and sugar, then add beaten egg. Stir in sifted flour. Dissolve baking soda in milk and add to mixture. Turn into a greased 20-cm cake tin and bake at 160°C for about 30 minutes. Ice with lemon or passionfruit icing.

Variation:
Replace feijoas with 2 mashed bananas for a tasty Banana Cake.

♦ PINEAPPLE TEA CAKE

100g butter
1 egg, beaten
½ cup milk
2 cups self-raising flour
½ cup sugar

pinch of salt
1 x 225g can crushed pineapple,
  drained
½ cup honey
¾ cup coconut

Melt half the butter and combine with egg and milk. Add to flour, sugar and salt. Pour into greased 20-cm cake tin, spread the drained pineapple over. Cream remaining butter and honey and pour over pineapple. Sprinkle with coconut. Bake at 180°C for 35-40 minutes.

♦ FUDGE CAKE (1)

1 tbsp cocoa
225g crushed wine biscuits
½ cup walnuts
75g butter, melted

1 tbsp sugar
1 tbsp golden syrup
50g chocolate, grated

Mix all ingredients except chocolate and press into sponge roll tin. Melt chocolate and spread over. Chill and cut.

17

♦ JAFFA FUDGE CAKE

100g butter
1/2 cup sweetened condensed milk
1/2 cup chocolate chips

grated rind of 1 orange
1 packet wine biscuits, crushed
1 cup coconut

Melt butter. Stir in other ingredients. Press into greased sponge roll tin. Leave in cool place to set. Ice with orange icing (p.34).

♦ AMERICAN CAKE

100g butter
1 cup sugar
1 egg, beaten

1/2 cup milk
2 cups flour
1 1/2 tsp baking powder

Topping:
100g chocolate, grated

50g walnuts

Cream butter and sugar, add beaten egg and milk. Add sifted dry ingredients. Put into greased 20-cm cake tin. Mix chocolate and nuts and sprinkle over. Bake 45 minutes at 180°C.

♦ CONTINENTAL CAKE

115g butter
1/2 cup sugar
1 egg, beaten
2 cups flour

1 tsp baking powder
pinch of salt
2-3 tbsp milk

Topping:
115g butter
1/2 cup sugar
90g ground almonds

2-3 tbsp milk
vanilla essence
almond essence

Cream butter and sugar, add egg. Add sifted dry ingredients and milk and spread in 23-cm cake tin.

For topping, melt butter in saucepan, add sugar almonds and milk. Bring to boil stirring constantly. Add essences and spread over cake base. Bake at 180°C for 45 minutes.

♦ BUFFALO CAKE

85g butter
1 cup sugar
pinch of salt
3 eggs

3 tbsp milk
1 1/2 cups flour
3 tsp baking powder
1/2 tsp vanilla essence

Cream butter, sugar and salt. Beat in one egg. Add the milk, flour and the other eggs. Fold in baking powder and vanilla. Pour into 23-cm tin. Bake at 190°C for 30-40 minutes.

♦ NORWEGIAN MOCHA CAKE

2 cups strong black coffee
2 cups sugar
1 tbsp cocoa
1 cup seedless raisins
200g butter
$1/2$ tsp vanilla
2 eggs

$1/2$ tsp ground cloves
1 tsp cinnamon
1 tsp nutmeg
2 cups sifted flour
$1/2$ tsp baking soda
2 tsp baking powder
pinch of salt

Combine coffee, 1 cup of the sugar, cocoa, and chopped raisins in pan and simmer 10 minutes. Cool. Cream butter and remainder of sugar, add eggs and flavourings and cooled mixture, and beat well. Sift in dry ingredients. Spread into 25-cm tin and bake at 180°C for 1 hour.

♦ LAZY DAISY CAKE

1 cup milk
2 tbsp butter
4 eggs
2 cups castor sugar

2 tsp vanilla
2 cups flour
1 tsp salt
2 tsp baking powder

Topping:
170g butter
2 cups coconut

4 tbsp full cream evaporated milk
10 tbsp brown sugar

Bring milk and butter to boil in saucepan. Beat eggs, gradually add sugar and vanilla and beat until thick. Add sifted flour, salt, and baking powder, and then the milk mixture. Put into greased dish sprinkled with flour, and bake 20 minutes at 180°C. Remove cake from oven and leave a few moments. Melt and blend all the topping ingredients and spread on to cake. Grill until brown – about 2 minutes.

♦ PRUNE CAKE

175g butter
1 cup brown sugar
3 eggs, beaten
$2^{1}/_{4}$ cups flour
1 tsp cinnamon
1 tsp vanilla essence

$1/2$ tsp nutmeg
pinch of salt
1 tsp baking soda
1 tsp hot water
250g prunes, cooked and well
   mashed

Cream butter and sugar. Add beaten eggs, sifted dry ingredients, baking powder dissolved in hot water, then prunes and syrup from prunes to make a soft mixture. Turn into a greased 23-cm cake tin. Cook approximately 1 hour at 160°C. Ice with soft white icing.

♦ CELEBRATION CAKE

225g butter *or* margarine
1½ cups soft brown sugar
1 tbsp treacle
4 large eggs
4 tbsp sherry, brandy *or* cold tea
grated rind of 1 lemon *or* orange
½ tsp vanilla essence
1½ cups plain flour
1 cup self-raising flour

¼ tsp salt
1 tsp mixed spice
pinch of nutmeg or cinnamon
2 cups sultanas
⅓ cup glace cherries
2 cups currants
1½ cups seedless raisins
⅓ chopped peel (optional)

Cream butter and sugar until light and fluffy. Beat together treacle, eggs, sherry, lemon rind and vanilla essence, just enough to break up the eggs. Stir a little at a time into the creamed mixture, alternating with the sifted flour, salt, and spices. Do not beat. Add the fruit and mix just enough to distribute evenly. The mixture should just be stiff enough to fall easily off the spoon. Turn into a 25-cm round tin lined with two thicknesses of greaseproof paper extending 3 cm above the tin. Level off the mixture and leave to stand for 1 hour. Bake 3-3½ hours in bottom part of the oven at 150°C. Leave cake in tin until just warm, then place on wire rack. Will keep indefinitely in a cake tin.

♦ BANANA CHOCOLATE CAKE

125g butter
1 cup sugar
2 eggs, beaten
pinch of salt
2¼ cups flour
1 tsp cream of tartar

2 tbsp cocoa
½ cup milk
2 bananas, mashed
1 tsp vanilla
1 tsp baking soda
2 tbsp hot water

Cream butter and sugar, add eggs and salt. Sift together flour, cream of tartar and cocoa. Fold into butter mixture, adding milk, mashed bananas and vanilla. Add baking soda dissolved in hot water. Turn into greased 20-cm cake tin. Bake at 160°C for about 1 hour.

♦ DIABETIC FRUITCAKE

2½ cups mixed fruit
125g butter
1¼ cups water
pinch of salt
grated rind of 1 lemon
3 eggs, well beaten

2½ cups wholemeal flour
3 tsp baking powder
1 tsp mixed spice
1 tsp cinnamon
1 tsp lemon essence

Combine fruit, butter, water, salt and lemon rind in saucepan. Bring to boil. Cool for 10 minutes. Add eggs to mixture followed by flour, baking powder, spice, cinnamon and essence. Bake in 20-cm square tin at 160°C for 1¼ hours.

◆ CHOCOLATE CAKE *(Foolproof)*

120g butter
1/2 cup sugar
1 egg
2 tbsp golden syrup
2 cups flour

1 tbsp cocoa
1 tsp baking soda
1 cup milk
1 tsp baking powder

Cream butter and sugar. Add egg and golden syrup and beat well. Sift flour and cocoa and add with dissolved soda in milk. Beat together until smooth. Add baking powder. Bake in lined 18-cm tin for 45 minutes at 180°C. Ice with chocolate icing when cold. Coffee or ginger and spices may be used instead of cocoa.

Biscuits and slices
◆ CHOCOLATE CLUSTERS

225g plain dark chocolate, broken
    into pieces

150*ml* cream
250-350g cornflakes

Put broken chocolate into basin and stand over hot water until melted. Remove from heat and stir in cream. Beat well. Gradually stir in cornflakes. Drop small spoonfuls on to greased plate and allow to set.

◆ GINGER CRUNCH

2 cups sugar
125g butter
1/4 can condensed milk
1/2 cup fresh milk
1 packet wine biscuits, crushed

1 tsp ginger
1/2 tsp vanilla
lemon icing
grated lemon peel

Put sugar, butter and both milks in a saucepan. Boil for about 10 minutes, until golden brown, stirring all the time. Remove from heat and add crushed biscuits, ginger and vanilla. Pour into a greased tin. Ice with lemon icing and top with grated lemon peel.

◆ ORANGE FUDGE

125g butter, melted
3/4 cup coconut
1/2 can unsweetened condensed milk

1 packet wine biscuits, crushed
orange butter icing

Mix all together and spread in a buttered tin. Ice with butter icing made with orange juice and rind. Also good with butter and brandy icing.

♦ BUMBLE 'B's

½ can sweetened condensed milk 1 cup coconut
1 cup mixed fruit 1 dsp cocoa

Warm the condensed milk then add to other ingredients and mix well together. Roll into balls and roll in extra coconut. You can vary this by adding peppermint or orange flavouring.

♦ FUDGE CAKE (2)

125g butter
1 egg, beaten
½ cup sugar

1½ tbsp cocoa
250g wine biscuits, crushed
½ cup walnuts

Combine butter, egg, sugar and cocoa in a saucepan and cook until melted. Add biscuits and walnuts, and return to stove for a few minutes. Put into greased tin. Cut into fingers after 10 minutes. Ice with chocolate icing if wished.

♦ CHRISTMAS FRUIT BALLS

½ cup raisins, minced
½ cup moist prunes, minced
1 large banana, mashed
1 tbsp golden syrup

½ cup chopped nuts
¼ cup crushed biscuit crumbs
chopped nuts, coconut *or* crushed
 cornflakes

Mix first six ingredient. Shape into balls and roll in chopped nuts, coconut or crushed cornflakes.

♦ PEANUT BUTTER COOKIES

125g butter
1 tsp baking soda
½ cup brown sugar
½ cup white sugar
1½ cups flour

1 tsp baking powder
½ tsp cream of tartar
1 egg
1½ tbsp peanut butter
½ tsp vanilla essence

Melt the butter in a saucepan over a low heat. Combine the dry ingredients in a mixing bowl and pour the melted butter over. Add slightly beaten egg, peanut butter and vanilla essence. Mix all ingredients together. Roll into balls. Flatten with a fork. Bake at 180°C for 15-20 minutes.

♦ BUTTERSCOTCH BISCUITS

125g butter
3/4 cup sugar
1 egg

1 packet butterscotch instant pudding
1½ cups flour
1 tsp baking powder

Cream butter and sugar. Beat in egg. Add instant pudding. Add remaining ingredients. Mix well. Roll into small balls. Press and flatten with a fork. Bake 10 minutes at 180°C. Try chocolate instant pudding, or caramel. There are many variations.

♦ KORNIES

125g butter
1 tsp baking powder
1 cup brown sugar
1 cup flour

1 egg, beaten
1¼ cups chopped dates
3/4 cup chopped walnuts
cornflakes

Melt the butter in a saucepan over a low heat. Combine the dry ingredients in a mixing bowl and pour the melted butter over. Add egg, walnuts and dates. Mix all ingredients well. Take teaspoonfuls and roll in cornflakes. Set biscuits out on a cold tray and bake at 180°C for 15-20 minutes.

♦ OATEN DATE/APPLE CRISPS

1 cup wholemeal flour
2 cups rolled oats
225g margarine
225g stoned dates or apples, chopped

2 tbsp water
2 tsp lemon juice
2 tbsp brown sugar
pinch of ground cinnamon

Mix the flour and oats together, then rub in margarine. Turn on to lightly floured board and knead until smooth. Cut in half and press one half in greased 18-cm square tin. Simmer chopped dates with water until soft, cool, stir in lemon juice, sugar and cinnamon and spread over dough. Cover with other half of dough. Smooth top and bake for 25 minutes at 180°C. Cut while warm into slices and leave in tin to cool. If using apples, increase sugar.

♦ BIRDSEED BARS

1 cup sesame seeds
1 cup sunflower seeds
1 cup coconut
1 cup chopped cashew nuts

1 cup sultanas
100g butter
¼ cup honey
½ cup brown sugar

In a large frying pan heat the first four ingredients, one after the other, until toasted and lightly browned. Mix with sultanas in a large bowl. Heat butter, honey and brown sugar to soft ball stage, then pour over mixture in bowl and mix well. Press into pan so mixture is 2 cm thick. When nearly cold, cut into bars. Store in airtight container.

♦ HEALTH BISCUITS

225g butter
2 tbsp golden syrup
³/₄ cup raw sugar
1 tsp baking powder

1 cup coconut
2 cups rolled oats
1 cup wholemeal flour
1 cup dried fruit and nuts

In a saucepan melt the butter, syrup and sugar. Bring the mixture to the boil and then add the remaining ingredients. Press mixture into a 20 x 30-cm sponge roll tin and bake 15-20 minutes at 150°C. Cut while warm.

♦ FRUITY PEANUT SQUARES

125g butter
³/₄ cup castor sugar
1 egg
1 cup self-raising flour

¹/₂ cup coconut
¹/₂ cup sultanas
¹/₂ cup peanuts
1 cup cornflakes

Cream butter and sugar. Add egg and beat well. Fold in flour, coconut, sultanas, peanuts and cornflakes. Bake in greased 20 x 30-cm sponge roll tin for 30 minutes at 180°C. Cool in tin. Can be iced if desired.

♦ CHERRY BISCUITS

Base:

125g butter
1 cup sugar
1 egg
1 cup flour

¹/₂ tsp baking powder
1 cup crushed Weetbix
1 cup coconut

Filling:

¹/₂ cup dried apricots
¹/₃ cup cherries

¹/₂ cup walnuts
1 cup sultanas

Topping:

¹/₂ cup butter
¹/₂ cup sugar
2 eggs

¹/₂ cup flour
¹/₂ cup ground rice

Base:

Beat butter and sugar thoroughly, add egg and beat again. Then add flour, baking powder, Weetbix and coconut. Mix well and spread into a greased 20 x 30-cm swiss roll tin. Place in fridge while you prepare filling.

Filling:

Chop fruit and nuts. Spread base with jam and cover with fruit and nuts. Cover with topping.

Topping:

Beat together the butter, sugar and eggs then mix in flour and ground rice. Spread over fruit and bake 30-45 minutes at 180°C. Ice when cold if desired.

◆ BEETLES

125g butter
³/₄ cup sugar
225g dates, chopped

1 tsp vanilla
4 cups rice bubbles
coconut

Slowly cook first three ingredients until soft, stirring until well mixed. Take off stove and add vanilla and rice bubbles. Roll teaspoon lots into balls and roll in coconut.

◆ FESTIVAL COCONUT SQUARES

1 cup coconut
1 tbsp icing sugar
¹/₂ cup milk
1 egg
³/₄ cup brown sugar, packed firmly

1¹/₂ cups flour
1 tbsp cocoa
1 tsp baking powder
125g butter, melted

Combine coconut and icing sugar. Add milk to make paste. Beat egg and brown sugar. Add sifted flour, cocoa and baking powder. Mix in melted butter. Spread half mixture in greased tin and spread coconut mixture on top. Cover with remaining mixture. Bake 30 minutes at 180°C. Ice when cold with chocolate icing.

◆ WONDER SLICE

1¹/₄ cups flour
³/₄ cup sugar
1 tsp baking powder
1 tbsp cocoa

1 tsp baking soda
125g butter
1 cup milk
1 cup dried fruit and nuts, mixed

Sift flour, sugar, baking powder, cocoa and soda. Melt butter and milk together in a pan – do not boil. Add to dry ingredients. Mix well. Add fruit and nuts. Spread into a greased 20 x 30-cm sponge roll tin. Bake at 200°C for about 20 minutes. Ice when cold and cut in squares. Can omit cocoa to make it plain – add 1 tablespoon extra flour.

◆ SHORTBREAD

225g butter
1 cup icing sugar
vanilla essence to taste

2 cups flour
1¹/₂ cups cornflour

Cream butter and icing sugar. Add vanilla essence. Gradually work in flour and cornflour. Make a long (sausage) roll. Chill. Slice into biscuits and bake at 160°C for about 30 minutes or until lightly cooked.

♦ COCONUT CREAMS

225g butter
³/₄ cup sugar
vanilla
1¹/₂ cups coconut

2 cups flour
2 tbsp cocoa
2 tsp baking powder

Cream butter and sugar. Add vanilla. Add dry ingredients. Add a little boiling water if mixture is too stiff. Roll into balls and coat with sugar. Flatten with fork. Bake at 180°C for 10-15 minutes. Put together with green peppermint icing.

♦ JAFFA SQUARES

¹/₂ cup coconut
¹/₃ cup cornflakes
1 tsp baking powder
1 cup flour

1 dsp cocoa
125g butter
¹/₂ cup sugar

Blend first five ingredients. Melt butter and sugar, pour over and mix well. Spread into 20 x 30-cm sponge roll tin. Bake at 180°C for 20-30 minutes. While warm ice with orange-flavoured icing. When icing set, add a layer of chocolate icing. Cut into squares before the biscuit gets cold.

♦ BONZERS

225g butter
³/₄ cup sugar
1 tbsp sweetened condensed milk
2 cups flour

³/₄ cup custard powder
¹/₂ tsp salt
1 tsp baking powder

Cream butter and sugar. Add condensed milk and beat well. Sift in dry ingredients. Either shape into oblong and slice into 1-cm slices, or roll into balls and flatten. Bake at 180°C for about 10-15 minutes. Store in an airtight container.

♦ LEMON OATMEAL ROUNDS

225g butter
2 cups brown sugar
2 eggs
3 tbsp lemon juice
2 cups flour
1 tsp baking soda

1 tsp salt
3 cups rolled oats
2 tsp grated lemon rind
1¹/₂ cups chopped dates
1 cup chopped walnuts

Cream butter and sugar. Beat in eggs and lemon juice. Mix in flour, soda and salt and stir into mixture. Add oats, rind, dates and nuts. Drop rounded teaspoonfuls 5 cm apart on tray. Bake at 180°C for 15-18 minutes until dry in centre, and edges well browned. Makes a lot.

◆ WEETBIX SQUARE

Base:

3¹/₂ Weetbix
1 cup coconut
1 tsp baking powder
1 cup flour

³/₄ cup sugar
50g butter, melted
¹/₄ cup milk

Caramel:

50g butter
3 tbsp brown sugar

4 tbsp condensed milk
1 tsp golden syrup

Base:

Crush Weetbix. Add dry ingredients, melted butter and milk. Press into 20 x 30-cm sponge roll tin and bake 15 minutes at 180°C.

Caramel:

Beat all ingredients together until smooth. Remove base from oven and spread with caramel mixture. Return to oven for 5 minutes. Melt on low heat and blend. When cold, ice with chocolate icing (p.34).

◆ NUTTY CARAMEL SQUARE

Base:

1 cup flour
¹/₂ tsp baking powder
75g butter

1 egg
1 cup chopped walnuts

Topping:

50g butter
¹/₃ cup golden syrup
1 egg, lightly beaten

¹/₃ cup firmly packed brown sugar
2 tbsp self-raising flour

Base:

Sift flour and baking powder into bowl. Rub in butter, mix in egg to make soft dough. Press in 20-cm square tin and cook at 180°C for 15 minutes. Remove from oven and sprinkle with chopped walnuts.

Topping:

Melt butter, remove from heat and stir in remaining ingredients until smooth. Pour over biscuit base and bake a further 15 minutes.

♦ BANANA BREAD

3 medium bananas	2 cups flour
1 cup sugar	1 tsp salt
1 egg, beaten	1 tsp baking soda
125g butter, melted	1 cup chopped nuts

Mash bananas and cover with sugar. Add beaten egg and melted butter. Add sifted dry ingredients and nuts. Pour into well-buttered loaf tin. Bake 1 hour at 180°C.

♦ CINNAMON TEA CAKE

2 tbsp butter	1¼ tsp baking powder
½ cup sugar	pinch of salt
2 eggs	melted butter
½ cup milk	1 tbsp cinnamon
1 cup flour	2 tbsp sugar

Cream butter and sugar, add eggs and beat well. Add milk, then sifted flour, baking powder and salt. Turn into greased loaf tin and bake about 30 minutes at 200°C. When cooked, cover top with melted butter, sprinkled cinnamon and sugar.

♦ PLAIN GEMS

1 tbsp butter	2 cups flour
1½ tbsp sugar	2 tsp cream of tartar
1 egg, beaten	1 tsp baking soda
¾ cup milk	½ tsp salt

Beat butter and sugar to a cream. Add egg, milk and dry sifted ingredients alternately. In a very hot gem iron, put a small piece of butter into each division. Put a tablespoonful of batter into each division. Bake at 220°C for 10 minutes.

♦ GINGER GEMS

1 tbsp butter	1½ cups flour
1 tbsp brown sugar	1 tbsp cream of tartar
2 tbsp golden syrup	1 tsp baking soda
1 egg, beaten	½ tsp salt
¼ cup milk	½ tsp ginger

Beat butter and sugar to a cream. Add the syrup, then the beaten egg and milk alternately with the sifted dry ingredients. Put in spoonfuls into hot buttered gem irons. Cook at 220°C for 10 minutes.

◆ OLD SAILOR'S RECIPE FOR CHEESE SCONES

125g butter
2 cups self-raising flour
125g cheese, grated

salt
pinch of curry powder
¾ cup milk

Grate butter, mix in flour and cheese, salt and curry powder. Mix with milk to form a stiff dough. Pat out or roll on a floured surface. Cut into scones. Bake at 220°C for about 10 minutes.

◆ SPICE LOAF

2 cups flour
2 tsp baking powder
2 tsp mixed spice
1 tsp cinnamon
½ tsp salt

25g butter
1 cup sugar
1 cup nuts and sultanas, mixed
1 egg, beaten
1 cup milk

Sift flour, baking powder, spices and salt. Rub in butter. Add sugar, nuts and fruit and mix together. Mix egg with milk, add to mixture. Turn into greased loaf tin. Bake at 180°C for 1 hour.

◆ SAVOURY MUFFINS

5 cups flour
1½ cups mixed vegetables
½ cup finely chopped bacon or ham
2 cups grated cheese
50g butter, melted
5 tsp baking powder

salt
1 onion or chives, finely chopped
3 eggs, beaten
1 tsp green herb stock powder
milk to mix

Mix all together with milk to make a soft dough. Spoon into greased muffin tins. Bake at 200°C for about 20 minutes. Makes 4 dozen.

◆ FRUIT MUFFINS

75g butter
1 egg, beaten
1 cup milk
1-1½ cups fruit (peaches, pineapple,
    blueberries, apricots, strawberries),
    cut into small cubes

2 cups flour
4 tsp baking powder
½ tsp salt
½ cup castor sugar

Topping:
1 tbsp sugar

½ tsp cinnamon

Melt butter, add egg and milk and beat to combine. Add with fruit to sifted dry ingredients. Don't over-mix. Put in greased muffin tins and sprinkle with topping. Bake at 220°C for 15-20 minutes.

♦ SPICED APPLE MUFFINS

1 cup flour
1/4 tsp salt
1 tsp cinnamon
2 tsp baking powder
1 1/2 tbsp sugar

1/2 cup peeled and grated apple
1 tbsp butter, melted
1 egg
100*ml* milk

Preheat oven to 220°C. Grease muffin tins. Sift dry ingredients into bowl and mix lightly. Add apple. Melt butter, add egg and milk, beat together. Make a well in the centre of ingredients in the bowl, add liquid and mix with a spoon. Do not over-mix. Place spoonfuls in tins. Bake 15-20 minutes at 220°C until golden. Serve buttered, warm or cold.

♦ BANANA MUFFINS

3/4 cup milk
1/4 cup oil
1/4 tsp baking soda
1 egg, beaten
1 cup mashed bananas

2 cups flour
3 tsp baking powder
1/2 cup sugar
1/2 tsp salt

Put milk, oil, soda and egg into a large jug, whisk until well mixed, add bananas. Combine dry ingredients in a bowl and add liquid mixture. Put into hot greased muffin pans. Bake at 200°C for 15-20 minutes or until golden brown.

♦ OAT BRAN CARROT MUFFINS

2 eggs
3/4 cup sugar
1/4 cup milk
1/2 cup oil
1 cup grated carrot
1/2 tsp orange *or* lemon essence

1 tsp baking soda
1/2 cup oat bran
1/2 cup chopped walnuts
1 cup flour
1 tsp mixed spice
1/4 cup chopped raisins

Beat eggs until frothy, gradually beat in sugar. Add milk and oil and beat. Stir in carrot and orange or lemon essence. Sprinkle baking soda over top. In another bowl mix oat bran, walnuts, flour, mixed spice and raisins. Stir in enough egg mixture to just moisten all dry ingredients. Fill greased muffin tins three-quarters full. Bake at 180°C until well risen and brown, about 15 minutes.

♦ PIKELETS

2 tbsp sugar
1 egg
about ³/₄ cup milk
1¹/₂ cups flour

1 tsp cream of tartar
¹/₂ tsp baking soda
1 tbsp hot water
1 tbsp butter

Beat sugar and egg until light and frothy. Add milk, flour, cream of tartar and baking soda. Mix well together. Add hot water and butter. Drop spoonfuls on hot greased girdle. Turn when bubbles rise and break.

♦ TEA ROLLS

1 dsp butter
¹/₂ cup sugar
1 egg, beaten
¹/₄ cup milk

2 cups flour
pinch of salt
1 tsp baking powder
icing sugar

Beat butter and sugar. Add egg and beat well. Add milk, sifted flour, salt and baking powder. Make into a soft dough. Twist into rolls or plaits. Bake at 220°C for 15 minutes. Sprinkle with icing sugar.

Pastry
♦ CHEESE PASTRY

50g butter
¹/₄ tsp salt
1¹/₂ cups flour

50g cheese, grated
pinch of cayenne
about 2 tbsp cold water

Rub butter into dry ingredients until like fine breadcrumbs. Add cheese and sufficient water to mix to a stiff paste. Turn on to lightly floured surface and roll out. Use for savoury pies, flans or for apple pie. Bake at 200°C for about 15 minutes, or as needed.

♦ ROUGH PASTRY

1 tsp baking powder
2 cups flour
salt

125g butter or lard
1 egg, beaten
milk to mix

Sift baking powder, flour and salt together. Rub in butter or lard. Mix with egg and sufficient milk to make a stiff dough.

♦ PASTRY

1 cup flour   1 tsp vinegar
125g butter   ½ cup milk

This recipe can be used for any pastry recipe. Quick and easy to make, particularly if you own a food processor. Blend flour with butter, add vinegar in mllk. Roll out and use accordingly baking at 230°C for first half of cooking time, reducing to 180°C for remainder.

♦ FLAKY PASTRY

175g butter *or* lard   1 tsp salt
2 cups flour   cold water

Divide the fat into four pieces. Put one portion into sifted flour and salt until like coarse breadcrumbs. Add cold water to make a stiff dough. Roll into a rectangular shape and dot on second portion of fat. Fold top and bottom to middle, sides to middle, and then top over bottom. Set in a cool place 3 minutes. Roll out. Repeat twice more, giving the pastry a half turn to the left at the commencement of each rolling. Cut and shape as required. Bake at 230°C for 15 minutes or as size of item requires.

Fillings and Icings
♦ RUM BUTTER

225g butter   1 tsp freshly grated nutmeg
2 cups sugar   4-5 tbsp rum

Soften butter. Add sugar and beat well. Add nutmeg and rum and mix well. Put into containers and use when set. This can be eaten with scones, on steam puddings, with mince pies and Christmas puddings.

♦ CHOCOLATE COATING FOR LAMINGTONS

2 cups icing sugar   2 tbsp strawberry jam
3 tbsp cocoa   1½ cups warm water

Sift icing sugar and cocoa into bowl and stir in combined jam and water. Dip cakes in to cover then toss in coconut. This is a runny icing and soaks into cakes well.

◆ MARSHMALLOW FOR CAKE FILLING OR TOPPING

1 cup water
1 cup sugar

1 tbsp gelatine
flavouring

Boil water and sugar, with gelatine sprinkled over, for 5 minutes (do not stir). Leave until cold. Whisk until creamy, then add flavouring. Pour over cake or into lined dish for filling in sandwich cake.

◆ ROYAL ICING

sieved icing sugar
$1/4$ tsp tartaric acid *or* lemon juice

2 egg whites, stiffly beaten

Gradually add icing sugar and tartaric acid to egg whites. Keep mixing until the icing forms peaks. If not to be used through icing tubes, add $1/2$ teaspoon glycerine.

◆ FROSTING (1)

1 cup sugar
3 tbsp hot water

2 egg whites

Heat the sugar and water together. Boil until it cracks when dropped into cold water. Brush the sides of the saucepan with cold water as the mixture is boiling. Remove from the fire and when it stops boiling, add gradually the stiffly beaten egg whites. Beat until it thickens. Spread over the cake.

◆ FROSTING (2)

$1^1/2$ cups sugar
2 egg whites, unbeaten

5 tbsp water
1 tsp syrup

Beat all ingredients together with a rotary beater, in the top of double boiler or in a basin over boiling water. Cook over boiling water for 10 minutes, beating constantly. When thick, remove from fire, flavour and beat until thick enough to spread.

◆ FUDGE ICING

1 cup sugar
$1/2$ cup milk

1 tbsp butter

Boil all ingredients for 8 minutes in a saucepan, stirring all the time. Pour into a basin, cool and beat until thick. For chocolate icing, add 1 dessertspoon cocoa to the sugar, before adding the milk. Other flavours may be used for variations of this icing.

♦ BUTTER ICING

2 tbsp butter   4-5 tbsp icing sugar

Beat butter to a cream. Add icing sugar and mix well together. If too thick add a few drops water. If not stiff enough add more sieved icing sugar.

♦ MOCHA FILLING AND ICING

$1\frac{1}{2}$ tbsp butter   4 tbsp strong coffee
$2\frac{1}{2}$ cups sugar $\frac{1}{4}$ tsp salt
$2\frac{1}{2}$ tbsp cocoa

Cream butter and sugar. Add cocoa, coffee and salt and stir until smooth. Spread between layers and on top of cake.

♦ CHOCOLATE ICING

$1\frac{1}{4}$ cups icing sugar   1 tbsp soft butter
1 tbsp cocoa   water to mix

Sift icing sugar and cocoa into bowl. Add butter and mix in thoroughly. Gradually add water to get a smooth spreadable icing.

♦ ORANGE ICING

$1\frac{1}{4}$ cups icing sugar   1 tbsp soft butter
1 tbsp finely grated orange rind   orange juice

Mix icing sugar, orange rind and soft butter. Add just sufficient juice to make a smooth, spreadable icing.

♦ AN EXCELLENT RAISIN FILLING

500g seeded raisins, 1 teaspoon spice. Cover with water and when boiling thicken with 1 teaspoon cornflour. Cool before adding to pastry.

♦ PRUNE FILLING *(no sugar)*

Boil and stone about 450g prunes. Thicken syrup with cornflour, add juice and grated lemon rind. Put chopped pulp back into thickened syrup and let cool.

♦ APRICOT FILLING

Mince 125g dried apricots, cover with water, and simmer until cooked. Add brown sugar or golden syrup to taste.

♦ APPLE FILLING

About 6 apples, peeled, cored and sliced finely. Simmer in least possible amount of water. When cooked add brown sugar to syrup to taste. Mix well to pulp. Bake between layers of pastry.

♦ APPLE CHEESE FOR TARTS

450g apples
1 cup sugar

75g melted butter
juice and rind of 2 lemons

Stew apples and sugar. Add butter, lemon juice and rind. Stir over a slow heat until thick. Pour into jars.

♦ DELICIOUS TOP FOR JAM TARTS

2 tbsp coconut
1 tbsp softened butter

1 tbsp sugar
1 egg, beaten

Combine ingredients and spread over tarts and bake at 180°-190°C until light brown.

♦ FILLING FOR FRUIT SQUARE

1 large apple
1 cup raisins, currants, sultanas
  or dates

a little lemon peel
3 tbsp brown sugar
1 tbsp spice *or* cinnamon

Peel, quarter and core apple and put it through the mincer with the fruit and lemon peel. Add sugar and spice and mix well.

♦ FILLING FOR TARTS

1 cup sugar
juice and rind of 1 lemon
1 egg yolk

1 tsp cornflour
$\frac{1}{2}$ cup water

Put sugar, grated rind and juice of lemon and egg yolk into a saucepan. Stir in cornflour and slowly add water. Place saucepan on stove and stir until boiling.

♦ LEMON HONEY

juice and grated rind of 2 lemons
2 eggs, beaten

50g butter
1 cup sugar

Put all ingredients into a saucepan and cook gently until thick and smooth. Do not boil.

♦ MARSHMALLOW FILLING FOR SPONGE

1 cup water
1 tbsp gelatine

1 cup sugar
$1/2$ tsp vanilla

Swell gelatine in half of water for 10 minutes. Add rest of water, heat until dissolved. Then add sugar and boil very gently for half an hour. Add vanilla and pour into a basin to cool. Then beat to a stiff froth and spread on cake.

♦ CHEESECAKE FILLING

125g butter
125g icing sugar
125g ground rice

1 egg
1 dsp flour

Combine all ingredients and beat until thoroughly mixed. Bake in pastry at 190°C until set and golden.

♦ MOCK CREAM FILLING

2 tbsp icing sugar
2 tbsp butter

1 tbsp boiling water

Beat all ingredients until thick.

♦ PASSIONFRUIT BUTTER

6 passionfruit
2 eggs

1 tbsp butter
1 cup sugar

Put all together in jug and stand in saucepan of boiling water. Cook 20 minutes, stirring with a wooden spoon. Seal down in jars. It will keep for months. Very nice for sandwiches, scones or sponges.

◆ CHRISTMAS MINCE *(for tarts)*

450g apples
225g raisins
225g currants
125g suet
125g lemon peel

450g brown sugar
1 tsp spice
1/2 tsp salt
juice and grated rind of 1 lemon
2 tbsp brandy

Mince fruit and suet. Mix in all ingredients, adding brandy last. Spoon into jars and seal carefully. This keeps well.

◆ CONDENSED MILK FILLING

Cream together equal quantities of butter and sweetened condensed milk. Add either minced dates, sultanas, preserved ginger or cherries, or a mixture.

◆ CREAM CHEESE FILLING

125g cream cheese
2 cups icing sugar

2 tbsp cream
50g chocolate, melted

Cream the cream cheese with a fork, add icing sugar, cream or top milk, and chocolate. Blend thoroughly before spreading.

Yeast Cookery

Yeast can be bought in a dry state or in packet form. Fresh compressed yeast should be pale and moist. Dark patches and drying show yeast to be stale and some of the cells will be dead, so throw it out. Home-made liquid yeast is quite satisfactory, but unless the housewife intends to use it regularly, it is simpler and more convenient to use the packet yeast. Dried yeast must be activated by soaking in a little lukewarm water for about 20 minutes before it will begin fermentation.

It is important not to skip any of the steps outlined in the method and keep ingredients warm.

Kneading is working the dough lightly with the knuckles, and folding it over to develop the elasticity. It is important to use only sufficient flour to prevent the dough from sticking to the board. If too much flour is used, it is worked into the dough and makes the resulting product dry and tough.

The rising time varies according to the amount of yeast used and temperature while rising. When the mixture has doubled in bulk the next step should be started immediately. If the mixture is allowed to rise any further, the resultant product is likely to have a sour taste; also there may be too great an escape of gas and the mixture will collapse when placed in the hot oven. Cover the bowl in which the dough is rising with a clean cloth, to keep it warm and prevent the mixture drying excessively on the surface.

♦ STANDARD RECIPE FOR BREAD ROLLS

4 cups white *or* white and
   wholemeal flour
2 tsp salt
2 tsp sugar

2 tsp compressed yeast
285*ml* scalded tepid milk
   (more if wholemeal flour used)

Put flour, salt and 1 teaspoon of sugar into a warmed basin and leave in a warm place. Cream yeast with remaining sugar and add milk. Make a well in the centre of the flour and add the liquid gradually, stirring all the time, to make a dough; knead dough well for 10 minutes or until smooth. Cover and leave to stand in a warm place until it has risen to twice its original size. Turn dough out on to a floured board and knead again lightly. Cut and shape into rolls. Place on a warm greased oven tray and set aside in a warm place to double their size. Bake at 220°C for about 15 minutes. Makes about 16 rolls.

To give a glazed crust to the rolls, brush them with a mixture of milk and beaten egg when they are still hot from the oven.

♦ VARIATION OF STANDARD ROLLS

All these rolls are made from the same basic mixture and are suitable for serving at breakfast, luncheons, or with morning coffee. They make a welcome change for packed lunches and certainly save time taken in making sandwiches. Stale rolls can be recrisped by dipping in milk or water and placing in a preheated oven for a few minutes. Small rolls make an excellent base for savoury mixtures for party-supper snacks.

♦ BREAD STICKS

Make bread sticks by rolling the dough 1 cm thick; cut 1-cm strips and roll with the palm of the hand into long smooth rolls about the thickness of a pencil. Cut in 22-cm lengths and place on a warm greased pan 2 cm apart. Bake at 200°C and when nearly baked reduce oven temperature to 180°C and bake until dry and crisp. These bread sticks are particularly good to serve with soup or salad, or with grills.

♦ CLOVERLEAF ROLLS

For cloverleaf rolls, shape small pieces of the mixture into balls and place three balls touching for each roll.

◆ SWEDISH BRAIDS

Shape small portions of the dough into strips about 15 cm long. Cut lengthwise into three and plait the dough making sure the ends are pressed together firmly and tucked underneath.

◆ KNOTS

Shape dough pieces as for Swedish Braids and tie a knot in the centre of each roll.

◆ BUTTERSCOTCH NUT ROLLS

Dough:

3 cups sifted flour
1 tsp salt
$1\frac{1}{2}$ tbsp dried yeast
1 tbsp sugar

1 cup scalded tepid milk
$1\frac{1}{2}$ tbsp butter, melted
$\frac{1}{2}$ cup brown sugar

Butterscotch mixture:

125g butter
$\frac{3}{4}$ cup brown sugar

$\frac{1}{2}$ cup chopped nuts

To make dough, mix flour and salt in a large bowl. In another bowl mix yeast and sugar together, and add lukewarm milk mixed with melted butter. Leave until mixture froths. Make a well in the centre of the dry ingredients, add liquid, mix thoroughly and turn the dough on to a lightly floured board. Knead until smooth and elastic, adding more flour if necessary. Place the dough in a bowl, cover and leave in a warm place to rise. When the mixture has doubled in size remove from the bowl knead lightly and roll out 1 cm thick. Brush the top with melted butter and sprinkle with brown sugar, roll up as for a jelly roll, and cut in 2.5-cm slices.

For the butterscotch mixture, cream together butter and sugar, spread in bottom of a baking dish, and sprinkle nuts on top. Place slices of roll on this mixture and allow to stand until the rolls have doubled in size. Bake at 200-230°C for 15-20 minutes. This mixture is sufficient to make 24 rolls.

◆ ALMOND PASTE FILLING

$\frac{1}{4}$ cup butter
$\frac{1}{4}$ cup sugar
1 egg

$\frac{1}{2}$ cup real almond paste, crumbled
$\frac{3}{4}$ tsp almond essence

Cream together butter and sugar. Add egg, almond paste, and almond essence. Mix these ingredients together until they are thoroughly blended.

◆ DOUGHNUTS

1 tsp salt
³/₄ cup sugar
2 tbsp butter
1 cup scalded milk
2 tsp compressed yeast
¹/₄ cup lukewarm water

4 cups sifted flour
1 egg, beaten
¹/₂ tsp nutmeg
oil for frying
icing sugar

Add salt, sugar and butter to scalded milk. When milk is lukewarm mix in yeast softened in water. Add 1¹/₂ cups of flour, beat and then leave to rise in a warm place until full of bubbles and very light. Add egg. Beat in remainder of flour and nutmeg, then knead dough well, keeping it as soft as possible. Return dough to the basin, cover it, and leave in a warm place to rise until bulk has doubled. Turn out on a floured board, roll to 2 cm thick, and cut out the doughnuts. Leave doughnuts to rise again for 20-30 minutes, then fry them raised-side down in deep oil at 180°C for 2-3 minutes. Remove, drain, and sprinkle with icing sugar. Makes 24 doughnuts.

Oil is at 180°C when a 2-cm cube of bread dropped into it browns in 60 seconds.

◆ YEAST DOUGH FOR DANISH PASTRY

275g butter
¹/₂ cup flour
1 sachet dried yeast
1 cup warm milk

3 tbsp sugar
1 egg
about 3 cups flour, sifted

Cream butter and work in first measure of flour to form a smooth paste. Wrap in paper and chill until hard. Mix yeast with 3 tablespoons of the measured warm milk and leave in warm place until frothy. Stir in sugar and remaining milk. Add egg and beat in well with wooden spoon. Beat in half the flour then gradually add remaining flour, beating until dough is shiny. Knead a few times then roll out to 35cm square. Roll out the firm butter on a floured board to half the size of the dough. Place on dough and fold dough over butter. Roll out to a rectangle. Divide dough into three and roll into rectangles from the open end. Chill dough if it starts to get sticky. Repeat rolling and folding twice more, then wrap in a clean cloth and leave in a cool place for 15 minutes. Make pastries, place on oven tray and leave in warm place for 15 minutes to rise. Bake at 230°C for 8-10 minutes. Makes about 1¹/₂ dozen pastries.

◆ FRUIT FLAN

Danish pastry is also suitable for fruit flan cases. Roll out the pastry dough to ¹/₂ cm thick, line a pie plate or sandwich tin with pastry, and fill it with jam or cooked fruit. Bake at 220°C for 20-30 minutes. If desired, the unfilled shell can be left until it has increased in bulk by half before filling, but if this is done it must be cooked at 250°C for 8-10 minutes.

♦ CRESCENTS

For crescents roll the dough ½ cm thick; cut with a sharp floured knife into 8-cm squares. Cut each square in half diagonally. Brush with melted butter and roll up from base of triangle to point. Twist the ends around to form a crescent.

♦ DANISH ALMOND CRESCENTS

Use Danish pastry yeast dough recipe above. Roll out the dough, ½ cm thick and cut it into triangles with bases measuring about 14 cm. Roll a little of the almond paste filling into a sausage shape and place it near the base of one of the triangles. Commencing at the base, roll it up to enclose the filling and bend it round to form a crescent, then place on a greased baking tray. Allow to rise in a warm place for 20 minutes. Brush over with egg and bake at 250°C for 15-20 minutes. While still hot, brush with glacé icing and sprinkle with chopped nuts.

♦ HOT CROSS BUNS

4 cups flour	50g currants
1 tsp salt	1½ tbsp dried yeast
1 tsp mixed spice	2 tbsp sugar
1 tsp cinnamon	300*ml* warm milk
50g butter	

Sift flour, salt, spice and cinnamon into a warm bowl. Rub in butter and add currants. Mix yeast and sugar, and add warm milk and leave until frothy. Mix all together and leave covered in warm place until double in bulk. Knead well and divide into 12 balls. Flatten and place on greased tray. Cover and leave 20 minutes. Bake at 220°C for 20 minutes. Brush with sugar and water and cut a cross in top of buns.

♦ EASY OVEN-RISEN BREAD

2 cups boiling water	2 cups wholemeal flour
2 cups milk	1 cup wheatgerm, rolled oats
2 tbsp brown sugar	*or* kibbled rye
1 tbsp dried yeast	1 tbsp salt
6 cups white flour	

Pour boiling water and milk into a large bowl. Mix in brown sugar. When lukewarm, sprinkle yeast on top. Stand bowl in warm water and cover and leave until frothy (about 10 minutes). Mix the flours, wheatgerm, and salt together. Add to the liquid and mix well with wooden spoon. Place in 2 well-greased 12 x 22-cm loaf tins. Put in a cold oven, turn oven on to 100°C and cook until risen, about 20-30 minutes. Turn oven to 180°C for about 40 minutes or until loaf sounds hollow when tapped. Makes 2 loaves.

◆ PIZZA PIE

Base:

2 tsp dried yeast
285*ml* warm water
1 tsp sugar

4 cups flour
1 tsp salt
2 tbsp salad oil

Filling:

450g cheese, grated
750g tomatoes, skinned and sliced
1 tsp marjoram

1 x 210g can tuna or salmon, drained
  and mashed
pepper

Sprinkle dried yeast into water. Add pinch of sugar and pinch of flour on top. Do not stir. Allow to stand 15 minutes or until it is frothy. Sift flour, salt and sugar into a bowl. Add yeast liquid all at once and mix with wooden spoon to soft dough. Knead dough about 5 minutes on floured board until it feels firm and elastic. Shape into ball and place in warm bowl. Cover and leave until double in size. Turn on to floured board and flatten into thin strip. Brush with oil and roll up as for Swiss roll. Continue flattening and rolling until nearly all oil is used. Cut dough in half and roll into two x 30 cm circles and lift on to greased trays, turn edges up and over. Spread with cheese, sliced tomatoes, chopped marjoram and tuna. Bake at 200°C for about 30 minutes.

◆ WHOLEMEAL HERB ROLLS

1½ tsp sugar
¾ cup warm water
1¼ tsp dried yeast
1 cup white flour
1 cup wholemeal flour
½ tsp salt

1 tbsp finely chopped parsley
  and thyme
1 tbsp melted butter
½ tsp poppy seeds, sesame seeds,
  or parmesan

Dissolve sugar in warm water, sprinkle yeast over surface and leave in a warm place for 10 minutes until frothy. Sift flour and salt into a bowl and put in a warm place. Add herbs and pour yeast mixture into flour, adding more warm water if necessary to make a soft dough. Knead on floured surface for 5 minutes. Shape into 9 rolls and place in warm buttered muffin tins. Brush with melted butter, sprinkle with seeds or parmesan and press lightly into surface. Cover with cling film and leave in a warm place 15-20 minutes until risen. Bake rolls for 10-15 minutes at 220°C until golden.

♦ CRUMPETS

2 tsp compressed yeast
1 tsp sugar
2½ cups warm milk

1 tbsp butter
pinch of salt
about 4 cups flour

Beat yeast and sugar to a cream, stir in warm milk. Melt butter and add with the salt. Sprinkle in sufficient flour to make a fairly thick batter. Cover and allow to rise for about 1 hour. Grease hotplate and drop spoonfuls of mixture on to it. Brown one side and cook about 5 minutes. After they blister, turn over and brown other side.

♦ YEAST BUNS

2 tbsp compressed yeast
1 tsp sugar
1¾ cups lukewarm milk
1¾ cups flour
125g butter
½ cup sugar

about 4 cups flour
2 eggs, beaten
50g peel
125g sultanas
pinch of salt

Cream yeast and 1 tsp sugar together, and pour lukewarm milk over. Leave to froth. Mix gradually into first measure of sifted flour and knead lightly. Leave to rise for 1 hour in a warm place. Cream butter, add sugar to second measure of sifted flour. When first mixture is ready, beat in remainder of ingredients alternately with flour mixture to get a soft dough. Leave mixture to rise for 1 hour. Turn on to floured board and cut into equal portions. Make smooth and round and place on a cold tray. Bake about 20 minutes at 230°C. When cooked, brush over with a syrup made with 2 tbsp sugar and half a cup water boiled for a few minutes.

♦ GERMAN COFFEE BREAD

75g cup butter
¼ cup sugar
½ tsp salt
1 cup scalded milk

1 tbsp yeast
1 egg, beaten
½ cup chopped raisins
4 cups flour

Strudel:
3 tbsp butter
⅓ cup sugar

1 tsp cinnamon
3 tbsp flour

Add butter, sugar and salt to the scalded milk. When lukewarm sprinkle over the yeast and leave to froth. Add egg, raisins and sufficient flour to make a batter, almost stiff enough to turn out and knead. Cover and allow to rise. Spread 1 cm thick in a buttered pan. Cover and leave to rise again. Before baking brush over with a little beaten egg and sprinkle with strudel mixture.

Strudel:
Melt butter, sugar and cinnamon and when sugar is partially melted, add flour. Bake the coffee bread at 180°C for about 30 minutes.

♦ CHRISTMAS STOLLEN

1½ tbsp dried yeast
¼ cup warm water
1 cup warm milk
2 tbsp sugar
½ tsp salt
4½ cups sifted flour
½ cup finely chopped candied peel
½ cup finely chopped glacé cherries
1 cup slivered blanched almonds

grated rind of 1 lemon
1 cup seedless raisins
2 eggs, well beaten
½ cup butter *or* margarine
¼ tsp nutmeg
2 tbsp melted butter
½ tsp cinnamon
1 tbsp sugar
icing sugar

Sprinkle yeast into warm water mixed with a pinch of sugar. Leave to froth. Combine milk, first measure of sugar and salt. Cool to lukewarm and mix into yeast with 1 cup of the sifted flour. Cover with clean towel. Let rise in a warm place until double. Stir in candied peel, cherries, almonds, lemon rind, raisins, eggs, first measure of butter or margarine, nutmeg, and then enough of remaining sifted flour to make a moderately stiff dough. Knead on a lightly floured surface until smooth – about 8-10 minutes. Roll into a 20 x 30-cm oval, about 1 cm thick. Brush with some of the melted butter and sprinkle with combined cinnamon and sugar. Make a lengthwise crease down centre of the dough and fold over. Place on a large greased oven tray. Push the dough into a crescent shape. With the palm of the hand, press down along the crease to shape. Brush with remainder of melted butter. Cover with a clean towel. Let rise in a warm place until double. Bake at 180°C for 45-50 minutes or until golden brown. Sift icing sugar over top.

Confectionery
♦ TURKISH DELIGHT

2 cups sugar
4 dsp gelatine
¼ tsp citric acid

1 cup hot water
raspberry essence
icing sugar

Put sugar, citric acid, gelatine and water in a saucepan and bring to the boil, stirring. Boil 20 minutes without stirring. Cool 10 minutes. Add essence. Pour into greased tin and leave 24 hours. Cut into squares and sprinkle icing sugar liberally on to each piece to prevent pieces sticking together.

♦ HOREHOUND CANDY (For coughs, colds, sore throats, congestion)

Into a saucepan place a good handful of horehound stems and leaves, with a cupful of water. Bring to the boil, cover and allow to infuse for at least 10 minutes. Strain. In a largish pan put 2 cups sugar, 25g butter, and ½ cup horehound liquid. Boil as for toffee, giving a stir occasionally before it comes to the boil and when thick, take off and beat. Pour on to greased dish to set. Cut while warmish as for fudge as it gets quite hard.

♦ HOKEY POKEY

4 tbsp sugar   1 tsp baking soda
2 tsp golden syrup

Bring sugar and syrup to the boil slowly stirring all the time. Boil for 7 minutes.
Remove from heat and add soda. Stir quickly and pour at once into greased dish.
Break in pieces when cold.

♦ MARZIPAN FRUITS AND VEGETABLES

225g icing sugar   1 egg, beaten
225g castor sugar   few drops of almond essence
225g ground almonds

Mix dry ingredients to a stiff paste with beaten egg. Add essence. Knead well in
a little extra icing sugar to make a stiff dough, break off portions and mould into
fruit or vegetable shapes. Use whole cloves as stalks and colour with food
colourings.

Cheese and Egg Dishes

CHEESE AND EGG DISHES

Cheese dishes

♦ SPAGHETTI AND CABBAGE WITH CHEESE SAUCE

³/₄ cup spaghetti, broken into pieces
  and cooked
1 cup grated cheese

1 cup hot white sauce
2 cups shredded cabbage
buttered breadcrumbs

Drain spaghetti. Add cheese to hot white sauce and stir until cheese is melted. Layer alternately spaghetti and cabbage in a casserole dish. Pour sauce over and cover with buttered crumbs. Cook for 40 minutes at 180°C.

♦ WELSH RAREBIT

Basic Recipe
1 tbsp butter
450g tasty Cheddar cheese, grated
¹/₂ tsp Worcester sauce

¹/₂ tsp dry mustard
pinch of cayenne
²/₃ cup lukewarm beer (measured
  without foam) or milk

Melt butter in top of double boiler over simmering water. Add cheese all at one time and stir occasionally until cheese begins to melt. Blend in Worcester sauce, mustard and cayenne. As soon as cheese begins to melt add beer or milk very gradually and stir constantly. As soon as beer or milk is blended in and mixture is smooth, serve immediately over crisp slices of toast.

♦ PASTA IN CREAM CHEESE SAUCE

250g spinach pasta
1 tbsp oil
50g thick bacon, finely chopped
1 tbsp butter
2-3 large onions, finely chopped
salt and black pepper

1 tsp marjoram
1 tsp cinnamon
1 cup grated cheese
125ml cream
paprika

Cook pasta in boiling water which has 1 tablespoon oil added to keep pasta separated. In a fry pan cook bacon in butter. Add onions, salt, pepper and marjoram. Over low heat combine in pot bacon mixture and strained pasta. Add cinnamon. Thoroughly mix in cheese. Add cream and heat through. Serve hot sprinkled with paprika to decorate. Serve with tossed salad.

♦ CHEESE AND NUT CROQUETTES

2 cups breadcrumbs
1 cup finely chopped nuts
1 tbsp chopped parsley
2 tbsp grated cheese
1 small onion, grated

salt and pepper
nutmeg
1 egg
milk to mix

Blend breadcrumbs, nuts, parsley, cheese, onion and seasoning, adding a little grated nutmeg if liked. Stir in well-beaten egg with just enough milk to make a stiff paste. Form into croquettes, bake on a greased dish for 20 minutes and serve hot with tomato sauce.

♦ CHEESE WITH TOMATOES

1 onion, sliced
6 tomatoes, skinned
butter or oil
1 tbsp milk

75g cooked macaroni
75g cheese, grated
salt and pepper
3/4 cup buttered crumbs

Fry onions and tomatoes in a little butter or oil. Mix milk, macaroni, cheese and seasonings and layer with onion mixture in a buttered pie dish. Sprinkle with buttered crumbs. Bake for 20 minutes at 180°C.

♦ CHEESE SOUFFLÉ

3 tbsp butter
3 tbsp flour
1/2 tsp salt
3/4 cup milk

1/2 cup grated cheese
1/4 tsp dry mustard
3 eggs, separated

Make the butter, flour, salt and milk into a thick white sauce. Stir in cheese and mustard until cheese melts. Set aside. Lightly grease a 3-cup soufflé or ovenware dish. Tie a band of greased greaseproof paper around it. Stir egg yolks into cheese sauce. Beat egg whites until stiff but not dry. Fold into sauce. Turn into prepared dish. Bake at 200°C for about 35 minutes. Serve at once.

♦ TOMATO CHEESE

25g butter
1 tbsp tomato sauce
2 1/2 tbsp grated cheese

few drops of lemon juice
pinch of cayenne
buttered toast

Melt butter with tomato sauce and stir well. Add grated cheese, lemon juice and cayenne. Serve hot on fingers of buttered toast.

♦ CHEESE HOTCAKES

1½ cups flour	125g Cheddar cheese, grated
3 tsp baking powder	1 egg
pinch of salt	150*ml* milk
pinch of dry mustard	1tbsp melted butter

Sift together the dry ingredients and add the cheese. Mix together lightly. Beat the egg, add milk and melted butter. Stir quickly into the dry ingredients. Drop spoonfuls into greased patty tins and bake 15-20 minutes at 230°C. Makes about 12 hot cakes. Serve immediately while hot and fluffy.

♦ CHEESE PUFFS

Filling:

50g butter	1 egg, beaten
50g cheese, grated	salt and pepper

Pastry:

1 cup flour	75g butter or lard
pinch of salt	water

Filling:
Melt butter in saucepan. Stir in grated cheese, egg, salt and pepper.

Pastry:
Sift flour and salt and cut in butter or lard. Add sufficient water to make a stiff dough. Roll out thinly, spread cheese mixture on half and fold remaining pastry over. Cover top with remaining filling. Cut into fingers. Bake in at 220°C for 15 minutes.

♦ CHEESE AND ONION TART

400g packet shortcrust pastry	1 large tomato, sliced
125g bacon rashers	salt and pepper
1 cup thinly sliced onions	2 eggs
225g processed cheese	1 cup milk

Line a 23-cm tart plate with pastry. Cook bacon until crisp, remove and crumble when cold. Add onion rings to bacon fat, cook but do not let them brown. Fill case with alternate layers of cheese, onion and slices of tomato, pepper and salt, then add prepared bacon. Beat eggs, add milk, pour over contents in tart. Bake at 200°C for about 10 minutes, reduce heat for another 30-40 minutes.

◆ CHOKOS WITH CHEESE FILLING

2 chokos
1 egg, beaten
$^1/_2$ cup grated tasty cheese
salt and pepper

pinch cayenne pepper
1 tbsp chopped parsley
$^1/_2$ cup breadcrumbs
extra grated cheese

Cut chokos in half lengthwise. Scoop out some flesh from each half to get a total of about $^1/_2$ cup. Add egg, cheese, seasonings, parsley and breadcrumbs and mix to a stiff paste. Put filling in choko halves, sprinkle with extra grated cheese. Place in baking dish with a little water. Cover dish and bake at 180°C until tender.

◆ CHEESE POTATOES IN THEIR JACKETS

6 medium potatoes
50g tasty cheese, grated
25g butter

1 egg, beaten
150*ml* milk
salt and pepper

Bake potatoes in their jackets. Scoop out the centre and mix with cheese, butter, egg and milk. Season with salt and pepper. Refill the cases piling up the mixture. Return to oven set at 190°C for 10 minutes or until browned.

◆ CHEESE AND COURGETTE QUICHE

Pastry:
50g butter
25g lard

1$^1/_2$ cups flour, sifted
2-3 tbsp cold water

Filling:
1 medium onion, sliced
2 tbsp vegetable oil
500g courgettes, sliced
3 eggs

150*ml* milk
salt and pepper
125g cheese, grated

Pastry:
Rub fat into flour until like breadcrumbs, add water and bind together. Wrap the pastry dough in foil and leave in fridge for 30 minutes. Roll out and put in quiche plate and leave for 15 minutes in fridge.

Filling:
Sauté onion in oil, add courgettes and cook for 10 minutes. Beat eggs lightly with milk and freshly ground pepper and salt. Put vegetables in flan, pour over the egg mixture and add grated cheese. Bake at 190°C for 30 minutes.

◆ CHEESE ROLLS

scone dough from 1 cup flour
2 tbsp grated cheese
1 tbsp butter

1 tbsp beaten egg
salt
cayenne

Make a light scone dough. Roll out thinly. Cut in pieces about 8 cm square. Mix all other ingredients and spread on top of scones. Roll up, place join down and bake at 230°C for 10-15 minutes.

◆ CHEESE FONDUE

5 eggs, separated
1¼ cups milk
1¾ cup soft breadcrumbs

¾ tsp salt
⅓ tsp dry mustard
225g cheese, grated

Add beaten egg yolks to milk, breadcrumbs and other ingredients. Fold in stiffly beaten egg whites. Bake in buttered custard cups at 160°C until firm. Can be baked in one large dish taking a longer time at 180°C.

◆ CHEESE TOAST

1 egg yolk
1 cup grated cheese
½ tbsp melted butter
salt and pepper

bread
squares of bread
2 rashers bacon

Mix first four ingredients and spread on squares of bread. Cover with bacon and grill in oven until brown.

Egg Dishes
◆ SCRAMBLED EGGS

In frying pan melt 1 teaspoon butter for each egg. Beat eggs until whites and yolks are mixed. Season with salt and pepper and add 1 to 3 tablespoons milk, or less if desired, for each egg. Pour egg mixture into hot butter and cook slowly. Stir until eggs are the desired consistency. Serve at once. Scrambled eggs may also be prepared in the double boiler, using the same recipe and method.

The secret of scrambled eggs is to stir constantly to avoid custardy result. For variation use chopped chives, parsley, bacon or tomato.

♦ EGG AND ASPARAGUS DISH

2 tbsp butter
2 tbsp flour
1 tsp mustard
1 x 340g can asparagus, liquid retained

milk
4 hardboiled eggs
cheese, grated

Make white sauce with butter, flour and mustard and drained liquid from asparagus made up to 2 cups with milk. Place asparagus into ovenware dish. Add eggs. Pour over sauce. Top with thick layer of grated cheese. Bake at180°C until heated right through.

♦ EGGS FLORENTINE

250g fresh spinach
$1/2$ tsp sugar
pepper
4 eggs

2 tbsp unsalted margarine
2 tbsp grated parmesan
100ml low fat natural yoghurt

Steam spinach. Drain well and season with sugar and pepper. Poach eggs. Place spinach in a heated dish, dot with margarine. Make 4 hollows for the poached eggs. Meanwhile, heat half the cheese with the yoghurt over medium heat, cook 2 minutes only. Spoon over eggs. Sprinkle with remaining cheese. Grill briefly and serve at once.

♦ SILVERBEET QUICHE

1 cup cooked silverbeet
$1/2$ cup cooked grated onion
1 cup grated cheese
1 cup milk

$1/2$ cup self-raising flour
2 eggs, beaten
pinch of salt

Combine silverbeet, onion and cheese and put in a well greased dish. Mix remaining ingredients then pour over vegetable mixture. Bake at 180° for 30 minutes. Leave to stand 15 minutes before cutting.

♦ EGGS AU GRATIN

25g butter
2 tbsp flour
1 cup milk
6 hard-boiled eggs
1 cup grated cheese

$1/2$ cup breadcrumbs
mustard
salt and pepper
buttered breadcrumbs

To make sauce: Melt butter in pan, add flour and blend well. Add milk and cook gently. Cut the eggs in quarters and place in pie dish. Add grated cheese, breadcrumbs, mustard, and salt and pepper to taste. Pour sauce over this. Cover with buttered crumbs and bake at 180°C until golden brown and heated through.

◆ SPINACH QUICHE

Pastry base:
1 cup flour
60g cold butter

about ¼ cup water

Filling:
1 kg spinach *or* silverbeet
1 medium onion, chopped
1 cup chopped spring onions
½ cup parsley
2 tsp fresh dill (½ tsp dried)
¼ tsp nutmeg

½ cup feta cheese *or* cottage cheese
¼ cup parmesan
4 eggs, beaten
salt and pepper
oil

Pastry base:
Chop butter into flour with a slow stream of water in food processor. *Do not overmix.* Chill dough for 15 minutes prior to rolling to line a 20-cm flan tin.

Filling:
Heat spinach until it wilts then drain and process or chop. Fry onion and spring onions and add to spinach. Add herbs, nutmeg, cheeses and beaten eggs, salt and pepper and mix. Place in pastry case and bake 20-30 minutes until just set: 10 minutes at 200°C, then a further 10-20 minutes at 180°C.

◆ VENETIAN EGGS

1 small onion
2 tsp butter
3 cups grated cheese
1 cup tomato pulp

salt and pepper
½ tsp Worcester sauce
½ tsp dry mustard
2 eggs

Chop onion finely and cook in butter until soft. Add cheese, tomato and seasoning. Cook over slow heat until cheese melts. Add beaten eggs. Stir and cook until it thickens. Serve on toast with bacon.

◆ ASPARAGUS AND EGGS

2 bunches asparagus
4 eggs

1 tbsp melted butter
salt and pepper

Boil asparagus until tender. Cut off tops and lay in pie dish with butter, salt and pepper. Beat eggs just enough to break the yolks. Pour over asparagus. Bake 10 minutes in quick oven and serve at once.

♦ CURRIED EGGS

2 apples, peeled and cored
2 onions
2 tbsp flour
1 dsp curry powder
salt

1 tbsp chutney
1 doz raisins
2 cups stock or milk
4-5 hard-boiled eggs

Cut the apples and onions into small squares. Fry the onions and then add the apple. Sprinkle with the flour, curry powder and salt to season. Add chutney, raisins and stock or milk. Cook until the onion and apple are soft. Cut the hard-boiled shelled eggs in halves, add to the mixture and heat thoroughly.

♦ MADRAS EGGS

2-3 onions
milk
$1/2$ tsp salt and pepper

$1/2$ tsp curry powder
eggs

Thinly slice onions into frying pan, cover with milk, add salt, pepper to taste and cook few minutes (best if a little underdone). Add curry powder mixed with a little milk. Make wells in mixture and lightly poach one or two eggs for each person. Serve eggs surrounded with a little of mixture on toast if liked. (You can keep adding eggs until mixture runs out.) Simply delicious.

♦ CREOLE EGGS

1 small onion
4 tomatoes
salt and pepper
50g butter
$1^{1}/2$ tbsp flour

$1/2$ cup milk
4 hard-boiled eggs
1 cup dry breadcrumbs
1 tbsp butter

Chop onion and brown in hot butter. Add tomatoes and simmer until onion is tender. Add salt and pepper. Make a very thick white sauce with half of the butter and all the flour and milk. Add tomato and onion mixture and stir well. Into a buttered casserole (using some of the second half of the 50g butter quantity) put one layer of tomato mixture, layer of sliced egg, then breadcrumbs. Continue like this, then top with 1 tbsp of butter. Bake at 200°C for 25 minutes.

♦ SCOTCH EGGS

350g sausage meat
4 hard-boiled eggs
a little flour

1 egg
50g breadcrumbs
deep fat *or* oil for frying

Roll the sausage meat out to about $\frac{1}{2}$ cm thickness and divide it into four equal parts. Shell the hard-boiled eggs, dip in flour and wrap each one up completely in a piece of sausage meat. Egg and breadcrumb each wrapped egg and deep fry them for 5 minutes. Cut the eggs in halves lengthwise and serve hot with peas or cold with salad.

♦ PUFFY OMELETTE

butter *or* oil
5 eggs, separated
5 tbsp milk, cream *or* water

$\frac{1}{2}$ tsp salt
pepper

Set oven for 180°C. Melt butter or oil in frying pan suitable for placing in an oven, turning pan to grease bottom and sides thoroughly. Pour off surplus fat. Beat yolks until thick and lemon coloured. Add liquid and seasonings. Beat egg whites, until they stand up in peaks. Cut and fold yolks into whites. Do not beat. When blended, pour into greased pan and cook slowly until bottom is brown, about 10 minutes. Place in moderate oven 180°C about 15 minutes to cook top of omelette. Fold omelette by creasing lightly and serve at once on hot plate. Garnish with parsley.

♦ FRENCH OMELETTE

Ingredients as in Puffy Omelette above.

Melt butter in frying pan. Beat eggs enough to mix whites and yolks. Add liquid and seasonings. Turn egg mixture into frying pan. As omelette cooks prick the bottom and sides to let liquid portion on top run underneath until all egg is cooked. When bottom of omelette is lightly browned, fold and turn out on hot platter. Garnish with parsley. Serve at once. Serves 4.

For eggs done to perfection use gentle low heat.

♦ SAVOURY OMELETTE

2 eggs, separated
2 tsp water
1 small onion, chopped and cooked

chopped parsley
salt and pepper
1 tbsp butter

Beat egg yolks and water. Add the beaten whites and onion, parsley, salt and pepper. Melt the butter in a small frying pan suitable for placing in an oven. Pour in the mixture. When brown underneath put into a hot oven to cook the top and serve at once.

Vegetables

VEGETABLES

♦ FRIED NOODLES (*CHOW MEIN*)

225g noodles
225g lean pork
1/2 tsp cornflour
1/2 tsp water
5 tbsp cooking oil

3 dried mushrooms
1 onion
10 spinach leaves
25g green peas *or* beans

Sauce:
2 tbsp soy sauce
2 tsp salt
dash of sugar

1/2 tsp cornflour
1 tsp sherry (optional)

Boil noodles until they are soft but not sticky (about 5 minutes). Drain in a sieve and rinse with cold water. Slice the meat, mix cornflour and water and rub meat with it. Mix sauce ingredients together. Heat oil until very hot. Add meat and stirfry. Add, mushrooms and vegetables. Stir and add sauce and noodles. When sauce thickens it is done.

♦ MINTED GREEN PEA AND EGG MOULD

1 1/2 cups peas
2 dsp gelatine
hot water
1/2 cup vinegar

1/4 cup sugar
pinch of salt
3 hard-boiled eggs, sliced
1/2 cup chopped mint

Cook peas, drain and reserve liquid. Make up to 1 1/4 cups with hot water. Dissolve gelatine in hot water, add vinegar, sugar and salt. Pour a little liquid into mould. When set arranged slices of egg and pour over a little more liquid. Set. Add mint to remaining liquid. Arrange alternate layers of peas and sliced eggs in the mould. Pour over remaining liquid with mint in. When set, turn out.

♦ GRILLED TOMATO HALVES WITH GARLIC

2 large ripe tomatoes
1 tsp melted unsalted margarine
1 clove garlic, crushed

4 tsp mixed herbs
2 tbsp coarsely grated fresh parmesan
parsley sprigs

Preheat grill. Cut the tomatoes in half and arrange on a baking sheet, cut side up. Mix the melted margarine with the garlic and herbs and spread mixture on to surfaces of tomatoes. Sprinkle thickly with cheese. Put under grill and cook for 10-12 minutes until the cheese is melted and golden brown. Garnish with parsley.

♦ CAULIFLOWER À LA GREQUE

1 onion, finely diced
2 carrots, finely diced
5 tbsp salad oil
$^{1}/_{2}$ tsp salt
black pepper
$^{1}/_{2}$ tsp coriander seeds
bouquet garni

1 clove garlic, whole
250g tomatoes, peeled and chopped
150*ml* white wine
1 medium cauliflower
1 tbsp lemon juice
1 tbsp parsley

Heat first measure of oil in heavy based saucepan. Gently cook onion and carrot until golden. Remove from heat and add salt, pepper, coriander, bouquet garni, garlic, tomatoes and wine. Mix well. Add cauliflower divided into florets. Return to heat and simmer gently with lid on for 10-20 minutes until cauliflower is just tender. Cool. Remove bouquet garni and garlic. Stir in second measure of oil and lemon juice. Check seasoning. Place in salad bowl with parsley sprinkled over. Chill lightly.

♦ COURGETTE SLICE

3 rashers bacon
375g unpeeled courgettes,
    grated coarsely
1 large onion, finely chopped
1 cup grated cheese

1 cup self-raising flour
$^{1}/_{2}$ cup oil
5 eggs, lightly beaten
salt and pepper

Remove rind from bacon and chop finely. Combine courgettes, onion, bacon and cheese, sifted flour, oil and eggs. Season with salt and pepper. Pour into a well greased slab dish. Bake at 180°C for 30-40 minutes, or until browned. Can be served with a tossed salad, vegetables or as a supper dish. Serves 4-5.

♦ CREAMED SPINACH

Wash spinach well. Cut up roughly and cook as for cabbage about 8 minutes. Tip into colander over saucepan and drain and reserve the liquid. Make white sauce using some of liquid and mix with spinach. A few drops of lemon juice and a dash of nutmeg improve the flavour. Celery, leeks and beans can also be served in white sauce, with the addition of cheese, parsley or a sprinkling of blanched sliced almonds.

♦ SAVOURY POTATO

cold mashed potato
finely chopped onion
bacon pieces

milk
grated cheese

Mix all together and put into a pie dish. Put some grated cheese on top. Cook about 30 minutes at 180°C. Quantities depend on number of people attending.

◆ BAKED CREAM ONIONS

12 medium-sized onions
salt and pepper
1½ tbsp butter
1 tbsp flour
1 cup milk

pinch of salt
pinch of sugar
1 egg, beaten
breadcrumbs

Peel onions, boil 10 minutes and drain well. Arrange in buttered casserole, season with salt and pepper. In a saucepan, melt butter and add flour, stirring well. Gradually add milk and cook until smooth. Season with salt and small amount of sugar. Remove from heat, add beaten egg, then pour over onions. Sprinkle with breadcrumbs and bake at 180°C for 20 minutes. Delicious and very good for colds.

◆ GOLDENROD BROCCOLI

700g broccoli, broken into florets
1½ tbsp butter
2 tbsp flour
½ tsp salt
⅛ tsp white pepper

¾ cup milk
3 hard-boiled eggs, separated
½ cup grated cheese
¼ tsp Worcester sauce
¾ cup mayonnaise

Cook broccoli in minimal amount of water for 5 minutes. Drain well and reserve liquid. In a saucepan melt butter and stir in flour, salt and pepper. Gradually add milk, roughly chopped egg whites, cheese and Worcester sauce, and cook until thick, stirring constantly. Add ½ cup reserved liquid from broccoli, remove from heat and stir in the mayonnaise. Arrange drained broccoli on serving plate, pour sauce over and sprinkle with egg yolk pressed through sieve. Serves 6.

Beans, cauliflower or asparagus can be used instead of broccoli.

◆ CARIBBEAN GREEN BEANS

1 x 500g packet frozen green beans
3 tbsp butter
1 tbsp minced onion

1 tbsp chopped green capsicum
1-2 tsp lemon or lime juice
salt and pepper

Cook beans lightly and drain well. Toss together green beans with other ingredients. Serve hot.

♦ MUSHROOM STROGANOV

2 onions, minced
3 tbsp butter
500g mushrooms, sliced
$^2/_3$ cup dry red wine
2 tbsp Worcester sauce
$^1/_4$ tsp sugar

$^1/_8$ tsp nutmeg
$^1/_8$ tsp cinnamon
2 cups sour cream
salt and white pepper
2 cups cooked rice
almonds and raisins to garnish

In a frying pan gently fry onions in butter until softened. Add mushrooms and cook, stirring, for 5 minutes. Stir in wine, Worcester sauce, sugar, nutmeg, and cinnamon. Cook over moderate heat until liquid is reduced by half. Add sour cream, cook mixture until heated through (but do not let it boil), add salt and pepper to taste. Serve stroganov over rice, garnished with sliced almonds and raisins.

♦ APPLE AND KUMARA BAKE

500g kumara
500g apples
1 tsp salt

$^1/_2$ cup brown sugar
$^3/_4$ tsp nutmeg
25g butter

Peel and slice kumara and apple. Layer in greased ovenproof dish, sprinkling each layer with salt, sugar and nutmeg. Dot with butter. Cover and bake at 180°C for about 1 hour.

♦ DEEP-FRIED CAULIFLOWER

cauliflower
1 cup flour
1 tsp baking powder
$^1/_4$ tsp salt

1 egg
$^1/_2$ cup milk
oil for frying

Break cauliflower into small pieces. Parboil in salted water and drain well. Mix all dry ingredients together, add egg and milk to make a smooth batter. Dip cauliflower into batter, then deep-fry. Serve immediately.

♦ CREAMED CORN

1 onion, sliced
1 tbsp butter
1 x 425g can creamed corn

sliced tomatoes
grated cheese

Fry onion until lightly browned in butter, add corn and mix together. Place in dish and cover with tomato slices. Top with grated cheese. Cook in oven at 180°C for about 20 minutes or until brown.

♦ VEGETABLE RICE CASSEROLE

1 cup raw long grain rice
2 medium onions, sliced
1 green capsicum or 1 cup celery
1 cup sliced tomato, fresh or canned

1 tsp curry powder
1 tbsp beef or chicken stock
3 cups water
100g butter

Put first six ingredients into a 1.5 litre casserole dish. Pour 3 cups water over and put butter cut in pieces on top. Allow to stand for 1 hour if time permits. Cook for 1¼-1½ hours at 180°C. Stir occasionally to distribute evenly. Leftovers can be combined with mayonnaise and fresh vegetables.

♦ VEGETABLE SAUSAGES

1 cup mashed potato
1 cup breadcrumbs
½ cup grated cheese
½ cup chopped onion

½ tsp Marmite or Vegemite
1 egg, beaten
flour or extra breadcrumbs
oil for frying

Mix all ingredients except flour together and shape into sausages. Roll in flour or breadcrumbs and fry until golden brown – about 20 minutes. Parsley may be added.

♦ GREEN TOMATO SPECIAL

green tomatoes
½ cup flour
½ tsp salt

pepper
oil

Cut green tomatoes crossways. In a container place flour, salt and a dash of pepper. Coat tomatoes thoroughly. Fry in a well-oiled frying pan, turning occasionally until tender. Serve immediately.

♦ COURGETTES AND FRENCH BEANS

500g small courgettes
500g French beans
250g butter

1 clove garlic, peeled and crushed
5 level tbsp fresh chopped parsley

Wash and slice courgettes lengthwise. Top and tail beans. Place beans in boiling salted water for 5 minutes, then add courgettes to pan and cook for further 5 minutes. Meanwhile, soften butter in bowl and blend in garlic and parsley until well mixed. Drain vegetables and place on serving dish. Melt butter in pan and pour over vegetables.

♦ CAULIFLOWER BAKED WITH MUSHROOMS

Break or cut cauliflower into florets and parboil in salted water. Drain well. Grease a casserole dish and place cauliflower in it with plenty of sliced mushrooms and lots of chopped parsley. Season with salt and pepper and pour in some cream. Smother with grated cheese and bake, uncovered, at 180°C for 20-30 minutes.

♦ VEGETARIAN PIE

6 medium potatoes, grated
3 medium carrots, grated
1 large onion, grated
1 clove garlic, crushed
2 eggs
2 tbsp oil
1 tsp salt

$^1/_4$ cup chopped parsley
$^1/_4$ cup breadcrumbs
1 cup milk powder
15g butter or margarine
1 cup grated cheese
yoghurt
4 spring onions, chopped

Combine potatoes, carrots and onions with garlic. Lightly beat eggs with oil and salt, and add to vegetables. Stir in parsley, breadcrumbs and milk powder. Spread into a well-greased 20-cm pie dish, dot with butter and bake at 190-200°C for 50 minutes. Sprinkle with cheese 15 minutes before cooking time is up. Serve hot or cold with a dressing of yoghurt blended with spring onions.

♦ ONION AND TOMATO CASSEROLE

500g tomatoes
2-3 onions
$^1/_4$ cup breadcrumbs
1 tbsp mixed fresh herbs

salt and pepper
30g butter
$^1/_4$ cup grated cheese

Slice tomatoes and onions and put in alternate layers in greased casserole dish. Sprinkle with breadcrumbs, mixed herbs and seasoning. Dot with butter and sprinkle grated cheese on top. Bake 30 minutes at 180°C.

♦ CHEESE POTATOES

6 potatoes, peeled and sliced
$^1/_2$ tsp salt
2 tbsp flour

$^1/_4$ cup grated cheese
$1^1/_2$ cups milk

Place a layer of potatoes in a large greased casserole. Sprinkle with salt, flour and cheese. Repeat and pour milk over top. Cover. Bake at 180°C for 1-1$^1/_2$ hours or until tender. Uncover for last 20 minutes of cooking to brown. If desired, add minced onion or tomato.

♦ ASPARAGUS AND SWEETCORN CASSEROLE

1 x 300g can asparagus pieces
60g butter
1 onion, chopped
2 tbsp flour
1 cup milk
450g whole kernel sweetcorn

1 tsp lemon juice
salt and pepper
2 hard-boiled eggs
chopped chives *or* parsley (optional)
potato crisps, crushed

Drain asparagus, reserve liquid. Heat butter in pan, add onion, sauté until tender; add flour and stir until golden brown. Gradually add milk and some of the asparagus liquid. Stir until sauce boils and thickens adding remaining liquid if necessary. Then add corn, asparagus, lemon juice, salt and pepper, eggs, and chives or parsley. Sprinkle with crushed potato crisps before serving.

Also can be topped with the following: 30g butter, 30g cheddar cheese, 1 cup fresh breadcrumbs. Heat butter in pan, add breadcrumbs and grated cheese. Mix well and sprinkle on sauce mixture. Bake uncovered at 180°C for about 20 minutes. Can be reheated.

♦ DELICIOUS VEGETABLE PIE

3 medium unpeeled courgettes,
    coarsely grated
1 large onion, finely chopped
3 thick slices of ham, cubed
1/2 cup cooking oil
1/2 cup pineapple pieces, drained
1/2 cup grated tasty cheese

1/2 cup grated carrot
1 cup flour
1 tsp baking powder
salt and pepper
chopped parsley
4 eggs

In a large bowl combine all ingredients except last two. Lightly beat eggs and add. Mix all together and pour into large greased oven dish. Bake at 160°C for approximately 30-40 minutes until golden brown. Serve either hot or cold with salad or vegetables. Serves eight. Use any vegetables that can be grated. Can be frozen.

♦ POMMES ANNA

No cook book is complete without Pommes Anna, surely the most extravagant and delicious way of preparing the potato.

Peel potatoes and cut into thin rings. Then soak in water for at least 10 minutes. Butter a covered casserole well and place the drained potatoes in layers, seasoning well, and dot lavishly with butter. When the casserole is full, spread thickly with more butter, cover tightly and cook in a slow oven for 40 minutes. Turn the 'cake', replace lid and return to the oven for a further 40 minutes. Drain off any excess butter and serve very hot.

♦ STUFFED BAKED POTATOES

Bake the potatoes in their skins. While still hot cut in half lengthwise and scoop out the centres in a bowl. Add a little melted butter, some grated cheese, chopped chives. parsley or other herbs, garlic, salt and pepper, ¹/₂ teaspoon tomato purée if you have it; in fact, anything you have to hand. A little chopped ham or bacon is very good. Mix well and replace mixture in the cases. Stuffed baked potatoes can be prepared in the morning and reheated for dinner without any loss to the taste, in which case dot with butter before reheating at 180°C for 20 minutes.

♦ POTATO CAKES

450g potatoes, boiled
25g butter
¹/₄ cup flour

1 egg
salt
egg or milk for glazing

Mash potatoes and add melted butter, flour, egg and salt. Mix well and turn on to a floured board. Shape into small flat cakes, place in a buttered dish and brush over with egg or milk. Bake at 200°C until pale brown. Cut open, butter and serve hot.

♦ POTATO OR PUMPKIN CROQUETTES

450g potatoes or pumpkin,
  boiled and mashed
1 dsp finely chopped parsley
salt and pepper

1 egg yolk
2 tbsp butter
oil for frying

Mix all these ingredients together well. Form into croquettes and deep fry in hot oil until golden brown. Drain on crumpled paper and serve.

♦ CRUSTY POTATOES

¹/₂ cup toasted breadcrumbs
4 cups grated potato
1 egg, beaten
1 onion, grated

¹/₂ tsp salt
3 tbsp butter
¹/₂ cup grated cheese

In a bowl combine breadcrumbs, potato, egg, onion and salt, and mix well. Grease an ovenproof dish, spread the mixture into the dish, dot with butter and sprinkle with cheese. Bake at 180° for 40-50 minutes or until golden brown. Serves 6.

◆ POTATO BACHETOM

750g potatoes
2 tbsp milk
2 tbsp butter
1 egg, beaten
185g cheese, grated

1 onion, chopped
pepper to taste
2 tomatoes, sliced
125g bacon, chopped

Cook and mash potatoes with milk and butter. Add the beaten egg. Add two-thirds of the cheese, all the onion and a shake of pepper. Put all into a shallow 23-cm ovenware dish. Top with tomatoes and bacon and the rest of the grated cheese. Bake for 20-30 minutes at 200°C.

◆ TASTY POTATO FLAN

Pastry:
1 cup flour
60g butter
$^1/_2$ cup grated cheddar cheese

1 egg yolk
2 tbsp milk (approx.)

Topping:
2 cups mashed potato
60g butter, melted
$^1/_4$ cup milk
2 tbsp mayonnaise
1 egg

3 bacon rashers, chopped
2 shallots, chopped
1 x 310g can creamed corn
$^1/_2$ cup grated cheese

To make pastry, sift flour into a basin, rub in butter, mix in cheese, egg yolk and enough milk to mix to firm dough. Roll out to line a 25cm flan tin. Prick base well and bake at 230°C for 10 minutes.

For topping, combine potato, butter, milk, mayonnaise and egg and mix well. Spread half over pastry case. Cook bacon until crisp, mix in shallots and corn and spread over potato mixture. Top with remaining potato mixture and sprinkle with cheese. Bake at 180°C for for 30 minutes.

Salads and Dressings

SALADS AND DRESSINGS

Salads

Steps to a good salad:
♦ See that lettuce and other greens are crisp. Dry well after washing, place in a container at the bottom of the fridge for several hours to become crisp.
♦ Rub the bowl with a cut clove of garlic for a delightful flavour.
♦ The dressing may be tossed with the salad or served separately. If tossed, do not add the dressing until a few minutes before serving, otherwise the salad will lose its crispness.
♦ Try dipping the edges of lettuce leaves in paprika for a pretty effect when lining a bowl or for individual cups.
♦ Kiwifruit are a help when decorating a salad and also add flavour to any tossed salad. Likewise feijoas, cape gooseberries, oranges and crisp pears enhance salads.
♦ The flavour of a salad should be interesting yet not muddled. Do not overdo the variety of ingredients. Herbs such as thyme, sage, marjoram, mint, chervil or basil may be added and will make your salad distinctive, but the flavours should be so elusive as almost to defy detection.

♦ HERB FLOWERS

Make your lettuce salads, coleslaws and fruit salads pretty, colourful and interesting by adding flowers from different edible herbs. Try the colourful bergamots, the red of pineapple sage, the blue of borage, the variety of colours of sages and marigolds (calendula), and the mauve-blue of chicory.

All add colour and a subtle flavour.

♦ FOUR PRAWN SALAD

4 large cooked prawns
1/2 head of lettuce
1 tbsp chopped spring onions

1/4 cucumber, sliced
1 tomato
2 tbsp vinegar

Peel prawns. Wash and dry lettuce, tear into bite-size pieces and place in salad bowl. Add the spring onions, cucumber and tomato. Sprinkle the vinegar over the salad and toss. Arrange prawns on top of salad and serve.

♦ TUNA SALAD

1 x 175g can of tuna
250g beansprouts
100g celery, chopped
50g green capsicum, chopped
1 spring onion, chopped

1 hard-boiled egg white, chopped
1 tomato, sliced
1 large apple, peeled and grated
vinegar
mustard

Combine all ingredients, except vinegar and mustard, in a bowl and chill for at least 15 minutes. Dress with vinegar mixed with mustard to lightly coat. Serves 4. This salad can also be used as a sandwich filling.

♦ VEGETABLE AND MACARONI SALAD

$1/4$ cup natural non-fat yoghurt
$1/4$ cup mayonnaise
$1^1/2$ tsp vegetable oil
$1/2$ tsp sesame oil
pinch of salt and pepper

1 tsp toasted sesame seeds
1 cup each blanched, sliced
   courgettes and carrots, chilled
1 cup blanched broccoli florets, chilled
2 cups cooked macaroni spirals

Combine yoghurt, mayonnaise, vegetable oil, sesame oil, salt and pepper and sesame seeds in a bowl. Mix with vegetables and macaroni and stir to combine. Cover and refrigerate.

♦ COURGETTE SALAD (1)

1kg small courgettes, thinly sliced
$1/4$ cup vinegar
1 tsp salt
2 tsp sugar
4 tbsp chopped onion

3 tbsp chopped green capsicum
3 tbsp sweet pickle
2 tbsp chopped parsley
$1/2$ cup salad oil

Cook courgettes in boiling salted water for 2 minutes. Drain and cool. Combine rest of ingredients in a jar. Shake well and pour over courgettes. Best made a few hours before needed.

♦ COURGETTE SALAD (2)

500g courgettes, sliced $1/2$ cm thick
3 tbsp salad oil
2 tbsp lemon juice
1 tbsp sugar

$1/2$ tsp salt
freshly ground black pepper
1 tbsp snipped chives
1 tbsp chopped parsley

Boil courgettes until barely tender in lightly salted water – do not overcook. Drain. Mix oil, lemon juice, sugar, salt and pepper and pour over courgettes while they are still hot. Cover and leave for at least one hour. Just before serving add herbs and mix thoroughly.

♦ COURGETTE SALAD (3)

Simmer courgettes until tender, cool and quickly slice into $\frac{1}{2}$ cm rounds. Combine with sliced tomatoes, onions and green beans and serve cold in French dressing.

♦ TOMATO SALAD

400g firm ripe tomatoes
1 clove garlic, crushed
3 tbsp oil
1 tbsp vinegar

1 tsp dried basil
salt and pepper
1 small onion or spring onion, chopped

Slice tomatoes $\frac{1}{2}$ cm thick. Combine all other ingredients except onion and whisk together. Put tomatoes and onions in a bowl, pour dressing over and chill. Serves 4.

♦ MARINATED CUCUMBER

1 cucumber
soy sauce

vinegar
salad oil

Peel and slice cucumber or leave unpeeled for easier digestion. Marinate in equal parts of soy sauce, vinegar and oil. No salt.

♦ ITALIAN VEGETABLE SALAD

4 tomatoes, quartered
$\frac{1}{2}$ cucumber, peeled and sliced
1 small green capsicum, sliced
100g button mushrooms, sliced
2 tbsp white vinegar
1 tsp olive oil

freshly ground black pepper
1 tbsp chopped fresh parsley
1 tbsp lemon juice
1 hard-boiled egg white, sliced
$\frac{1}{2}$ head lettuce

Toss tomato, cucumber, capsicum and mushrooms in a bowl with vinegar, oil and black pepper. Refrigerate for 30 minutes. Add parsley and mix. Sprinkle with lemon juice, garnish with egg white and serve on a bed of lettuce. Serves 2 to 4.

♦ LAYER IN A BOWL

lettuce leaves
chopped tomato
sliced crab sticks

beansprouts
sliced bananas

Pour lemon juice over the top.

♦ WALDORF SALAD

1 cup diced dessert apples
juice of 1/2 lemon
1/2 cup diced celery heart
1/2 cup chopped walnuts

1/2 cup mayonnaise *or* French dressing
pepper and salt
lettuce leaves

Turn the apple over and over in the lemon juice to prevent discolouring. Mix with other ingredients except lettuce leaves. Season very lightly and chill, covered. Serve on crisp lettuce leaves.

♦ CAULIFLOWER SALAD

1 cup grated raw cauliflower
1 cup grated pear *or* apple
1 cup grated carrot
2-3 cups torn lettuce

2 tsp chopped parsley
2 tsp chopped chives
peas (optional)
French dressing *or* mayonnaise

Toss all ingredients together in French dressing or mayonnaise. Chill.

♦ COTTAGE CHEESE AND CUCUMBER SALAD

1 lime jelly
1 cup hot water
1 cucumber

1/2 cup mayonnaise
500g cottage cheese, creamed
pinch of salt

Dissolve jelly in hot water. Peel cucumber and slice lengthwise in 4 or 5 pieces and then slice each piece crosswise into small pieces. Mix all ingredients together, put into mould and chill until firm.

♦ COTTAGE CHEESE AND TOMATO SALAD

1 cup cottage cheese
1 tsp grated onion *or* chives

2 tbsp chopped green capsicum
salt and pepper

Garnish:
1 lettuce
1 tomato, sliced
mayonnaise

parsley
green capsicum, finely chopped

Blend first four ingredients together, cover and set in refrigerator 30 minutes. Shred lettuce or use lettuce leaves. Place two thick slices of tomato on lettuce and pile cottage cheese mixture on top. Serve with mayonnaise and garnish with parsley and capsicum. Serves 5.

◆ STUFFED TOMATOES

Hollow out medium-sized tomatoes and stuff with cottage cheese mixture described in the previous recipe, garnish and serve on lettuce.

◆ POTATO SALAD

450-670g potatoes
2 tbsp olive oil

2 tbsp tarragon vinegar
salt and pepper

Choose waxy potatoes for preference and barely cook them in their jackets. Peel and dice them and chop them into oil and vinegar while still hot. Turn the potatoes over and over in this dressing so that they will absorb the vinegar. Season to taste. Cover and chill.

Other suggestions: Add chopped spring onions including the green, and sprinkle generously with parsley. Use parsley alone. Add chopped green or red capsicum.

◆ CUCUMBER AND CARROT JELLIED SALAD

1 lime jelly
1 dsp gelatine
2 cups warm water
1 x 440g can pineapple pieces,
    juice retained
1/4 cup white vinegar

juice of 1 lemon
1 cup chopped celery
1 green cucumber
1/2 cup grated carrot
salt and pepper

Dissolve jelly and gelatine in warm water. When cool, add pineapple juice, vinegar and lemon juice. Cool until egg white consistency. Cut celery and cucumber, add grated carrot and fold in with pineapple to jelly. Season to taste. Pour into mould. Chill and serve on a bed of lettuce.

◆ WINTER SALAD

2 cups cubed apple
2 cups cubed pineapple
2 cups cubed cheese

1 cup chopped ham
mayonnaise

Place all ingredients in bowl and mix, using just sufficient mayonnaise to lightly coat other ingredients.

♦ GREEN BEAN SALAD

1kg young green beans, sliced
$\frac{1}{2}$ cup oil
2 large onions, chopped
4 hard-boiled eggs
2 sticks celery, sliced

$\frac{1}{4}$ cup chopped walnuts
small parsley sprigs
2 tbsp cider vinegar
salt

Boil beans in salted water until barely tender. Drain. Heat some of the oil and sauté onions until tender or lightly golden. Combine beans and onions in salad bowl; sieve eggs over, add chopped celery, and nuts, sprigs parsley, add remaining oil, and vinegar and salt. Toss lightly. Serves 6.

♦ KIWI SALAD (1)

$\frac{1}{2}$ lettuce
3 small courgettes
3 kiwifruit
3 sticks celery
2 tbsp oil

$\frac{1}{4}$ cup lemon juice
salt and pepper
pinch of tarragon
30g pistachio nuts

Prepare lettuce and chop coarsely. Wash and slice courgettes. Peel and slice kiwifruit and wash and chop celery. Mix the oil, lemon juice, salt, pepper and tarragon. Add the prepared vegetables and toss with the dressing. Chill and serve with a sprinkle of the pistachio nuts.

♦ KIWI SALAD (2)

1 lettuce, shredded
2 oranges, segmented
4 kiwifruit, thinly sliced
2 apricots, sliced

2 peaches, sliced
115g walnuts
115g tasty cheese, cubed

Dressing:
2 tbsp sour cream
2 tbsp salad oil
1 tbsp white or cider vinegar

pinch of salt
pinch of cayenne

To make up dressing, tip all dressing ingredients into a screw-top jar and shake until mixed.

Toss lettuce in half of the dressing in a salad bowl. Arrange the fruit in layers around dish, add nuts and cheese to centre of dish. Pour remaining dressing over cheese and nuts. This makes a most delicious salad with a very distinctive flavour of its own.

♦ SWEET 'N' SPICY SALAD

250g small brussel sprouts,
   fresh or frozen
3 firm tomatoes, cut into 4 or 6

1 small onion, chopped
1 x 125g can pineapple chunks

Dressing:
60*ml* salad oil
30*ml* lemon juice

$\frac{1}{2}$ tsp curry powder
$\frac{1}{2}$ tsp sugar

Combine dressing ingredients in a screw-top jar and shake until thoroughly mixed. Cook sprouts in salted water until tender, about 7 minutes. Drain and run under cold water until quite cold. Drain well. Toss sprouts, tomatoes, onion and pineapple in a serving bowl. Pour dressing over salad and refrigerate until ready to serve.

♦ CHEESE AND GRAPE SALAD

$\frac{1}{2}$ unpeeled green cucumber,
   thinly sliced
2 spring onions, sliced finely
225g black grapes, halved and
   de-seeded
1 x 440g can pineapple cubes,
   juice drained

125g cheese, cubed
60*ml* oil
30*ml* vinegar
ground black pepper
4 hard-boiled eggs, peeled
   and quartered

Arrange cucumber slices to cover the base of a large plate or individual plates. Mix onion, grapes and pineapple with cheese, oil, vinegar and pepper. Place in centre of plate on top of cucumber. Arrange eggs around the outside of plate just before serving.

♦ GREEN BEAN AND TOMATO SALAD

45*ml* oil
45*ml* vinegar
1 garlic clove, crushed
pinch of sugar
pinch of dry mustard

salt and pepper
4-6 medium tomatoes
250g cooked green beans
lettuce leaves
several fresh basil leaves

Combine oil, vinegar, garlic, sugar, mustard, salt and pepper in a small jar, shake well and chill. Slice firm tomatoes and mix with beans and chill. Line a salad bowl with pieces of lettuce. Pour the dressing over the vegetables and carefully toss. Pile into bowl and sprinkle with sweet basil. Serve on lettuce leaves. A summer salad with a difference.

♦ SUMMER SALAD

lettuce
beetroot
mustard and cress
tomatoes

radishes
celery
spring onions *or* red onions
French dressing

All the above may be used. Wash, pick and dry the salad. Slice with a stainless knife or tear with the fingers. Place the French dressing in a bowl and toss the salad in it. Arrange in salad bowl and garnish with tomato, beetroot or egg.

♦ AMERICAN COLESLAW

1 medium cabbage, thinly shredded
1 tsp salt

1 red capsicum, chopped small
1 carrot, chopped small

Dressing:
1 cup cider vinegar
2 cups sugar
$^1/_2$ cup water

1 tsp mustard seed
1 tsp celery seed

Sprinkle salt over cabbage and leave 1 hour. Squeeze cabbage well, in fact very well, and add capsicum and carrot. Boil dressing for 1 minute then cool. Pour over cabbage mixture. Will keep 3 weeks in fridge but freezes beautifully. The secret is squeezing as much moisture as possible from cabbage.

♦ ORCHARD SALAD

1 x 440g can pineapple pieces
50g sultanas
125g celery, chopped

1 unpeeled red apple, chopped
45g blanched almonds
45g brazil nuts, chopped

Dressing:
$^1/_4$ tsp mixed spice
5*ml* lemon juice

15*ml* oil
30*ml* sour cream

Drain pineapple well and place in bowl. Soak sultanas in pineapple juice for 15 minutes. Then drain and add to pineapple pieces. Stir in the chopped celery and apple. Sprinkle nuts over salad.

Dressing:
Combine spice, oil and lemon juice in a screw-top jar, secure lid and shake well. Stir this into the sour cream. Dressing may be served separately if wished.

Salad Dressings

◆ FRENCH DRESSING

The usual proportion of vinegar to oil for a French dressing is 1 tablespoon vinegar to 3 tablespoons oil. Put vinegar into bowl or jar with cover, and add ½ tsp each of salt, sugar, a touch of French mustard and a good screw of pepper from the mill. Add oil and beat up with a fork or shake in jar. When the mixture thickens it indicates that the dressing has the right amount of oil and vinegar and should only require tasting to correct the seasoning. Onion, garlic or chives are added to taste.

◆ WHIPPED CREAM DRESSING

½ cup cream
¼ tsp salt

3 tbsp vinegar *or* 2 tbsp lemon juice
pepper

Beat cream until stiff, using an egg beater. Beat in other ingredients very slowly.

◆ ECONOMICAL BOILED SALAD DRESSING

2 tbsp sugar
25g butter
1 tbsp flour
½ cup milk
2 eggs, beaten

½ tsp mustard
½ tsp salt
½ tsp nutmeg
pinch of cayenne
¼ cup vinegar

Blend the sugar and butter in a double boiler. Add flour, then milk and eggs, seasonings and vinegar. Stir until it thickens and pour into jars. Thin down with cream or milk when required. Refrigerate.

◆ CONDENSED MILK SALAD DRESSING

2 eggs
1 tsp mustard
1 tsp salt

1 large can sweetened condensed milk
1 condensed milk can of vinegar

Beat eggs thoroughly. Add mustard, salt, condensed milk. Add vinegar and beat all well together. Keep in large screw-topped jar.

◆ EGGLESS MAYONNAISE

1 cup evaporated milk
1 tsp salt
¼ cup lemon juice

1 cup oil
¼ cup sugar
1 tsp mustard

Put all ingredients in electric blender and blend until smooth. Makes 3 cups.

Fish and
Shellfish

FISH AND SHELLFISH

◆ BAKED STUFFED FISH

Scale the fish. Remove the head. Cut off tail. Cut around fins and remove them. Slit fish open from head to tail along belly. Remove entrails. To remove backbone cut down to it, through flesh, on each side of fish.

Break the backbone by bending the fish. Cut out backbone. Small bits of flesh adhering to backbone may be added to stuffing (see Bread Stuffing p.140). Wash and dry the fish. Sprinkle inside and out with salt. Stuff fish loosely with dressing. Sew, tie, or skewer cut edges together. Place fish in greased pan. Brush with melted fat or wrap in aluminium foil to retain juices and flavour. Bake at 180°C for 40-60 minutes, or until fish flakes easily when tested with a fork. Baste with melted fat during baking if fish is dry. Serve on hot platter with garnishes, plain or with a sauce.

◆ BAKED FILLETS OF FISH

Soak fillets for 3 minutes in ¼ cup milk with 1 teaspoon salt. Drain. Place in greased pan. Cover fillets with breadcrumbs. Sprinkle with melted butter and lemon juice. Bake at 230-260°C until cooked, about 15 minutes. Grated cheese may be sprinkled over top of fish just before removing from oven. Use an ovenware dish to save time in serving.

Try this with a little white wine added in the cooking.

◆ GRILLED FISH

Clean the fish. Sprinkle with salt and a few drops of lemon juice or vinegar. If fish is very lacking in fat, brush with melted butter. Place in preheated grilling pan, or in oven at 230°C, cooking cut side first for about 6 minutes. Turn fish carefully to prevent breaking and grill other side – 10-12 minutes should be enough for total cooking time, depending on thickness of fish.

◆ BAKED SALMON or TROUT

Allow 450g salmon for three people. Wrap fish in well-oiled aluminium foil or greaseproof paper. Stand in greased baking dish, bake according to following timetables at 180°C: 225g for 35 minutes; 450g for 50 minutes; 675g for 70 minutes; up to 1.8kg for 2½ hours. Serve hot with hollandaise sauce or cold with mayonnaise.

◆ BARBECUED HAPUKA STEAKS

6 pieces foil to wrap fish
1 tbsp soft butter
6 hapuka steaks
1 cup grated cheese

1 medium onion, finely chopped
salt and pepper
2-3 tsp lemon juice *or* 1 tbsp sherry

Grease each piece of foil liberally with butter. Place fish on each piece of foil and sprinkle a little cheese and onion, and salt and pepper. Sprinkle with sherry or lemon juice and more cheese and onion. Wrap each parcel and seal well. Cook over hot barbecue for 15 minutes turning frequently. Serve with tossed salad and garlic bread. Thick boned fillets of snapper may be used.

◆ FISH WITH MUSHROOMS

4 fish steaks
185g mushrooms, sliced
4 tomatoes, skinned and sliced
1 clove garlic, crushed

2 tbsp white wine
1 tbsp lemon juice
salt and pepper
chopped parsley to garnish

Place the fish steaks in a well-greased ovenproof dish. Top with the mushrooms, tomatoes and garlic.

Pour over the wine, lemon juice and season well with salt and pepper. Cover with foil and cook at 180°C for 30 minutes. Garnish with chopped parsley. Serves 4.

◆ TAIL END OF FISH IN TOMATO AND GARLIC SAUCE

6 tomatoes *or* 1 cup tomato pulp
1 clove garlic
salt and pepper
$1/4$ cup white wine
finely chopped parsley

1 kg groper tail ends
breadcrumbs
butter
lemon

Cut tomatoes in pieces, add garlic, salt, pepper, wine and parsley. Cook 10 minutes, pound well, and strain. Put fish in pan, pour sauce over and cook gently for 3-5 minutes each side. Baste well. Place in ovenware dish. Cook at 160°C, basting several times, for 30-40 minutes. Cover with soft breadcrumbs, dot with butter and brown under top element. Garnish with lemon.

◆ POACHED SALMON or TROUT

Allow 450g for three good portions. Have pan just large enough to hold pieces of salmon. Cover with water, add peppercorns and salt. Heat almost to boiling point and hold that temperature using table above for times of cooking. Serve hot with hollandaise sauce or cold with mayonnaise.

♦ GRILLED SALMON STEAKS

Allow one steak about 2 cm thick for each person. Heat grill, allow 6 minutes grilling on one side, then turn carefully and grill for another 4 minutes. Season and serve.

♦ CURRIED CRAYFISH

1 tsp minced onion	2 tsp curry powder
1 tsp butter	2 cups weak stock
1/2 tsp salt	2 cups diced crayfish

Fry onion in butter. Add salt, curry and stock. Cook gently for 5 minutes before putting in crayfish. Serve as soon as this is thoroughly heated with boiled rice.

♦ TROUT

- ♦ Small trout may be baked in a fireproof dish in oven with butter and lemon juice, allspice, mace and salt. Baste several times in cooking.
- ♦ Freshly caught trout is at its best fried gently in butter or olive oil, with lemon juice, salt and pepper.
- ♦ Trout may be dipped in egg and breadcrumbs and fried gently in butter or olive oil.

Soused trout
This is delicious eaten cold. Clean trout and cut in thick slices. Lay them in a baking dish with grated onion, chopped parsley, dabs of butter and vinegar, grapefruit or lemon juice. Cover with greased paper or aluminium foil and bake at 180°C for about 15 minutes. Leave to cool in liquid.

Trout cooked in wine
Inside a cleaned trout place butter with chopped herbs (marjoram, parsley, thyme). Place fish in ovenproof dish and dust with salt and pepper. Pour over 1/2 bottle white wine, cook at 200°C for 25 minutes. The wine will have reduced a little. Add a little more melted butter, stir in, cook another 5 minutes. This is delicious hot and equally delicious cold with a crisp salad. Omit melted butter if trout is to be eaten cold.

♦ CHEESE FISH STEAKS

4 fish steaks	2 tsp dry mustard
butter	salt and pepper
1 1/2 cups grated tasty cheese	3 tbsp cream

Butter an ovenware dish (3 cup size) and place the trimmed fish in the bottom. Mix cheese, mustard, salt and pepper with cream. Spread over the upper surfaces of the fish. Bake at 180°C for 20 minutes. If cheese becomes too brown, cover with butter paper. Serves 4.

◆ KING NEPTUNE PIE

30g butter
2 tbsp flour
1 cup milk
2 tsp chicken stock powder

1 x 425g can tuna *or* fish fillets, drained
2 tsp lemon juice
1 cup cooked peas

Topping:
3 medium potatoes, cooked
and mashed

½ small onion, grated (optional)

Melt butter in saucepan, add flour and cook 1 minute. Gradually add milk, stirring constantly until sauce boils. Add stock, fish, lemon juice and peas. Season to taste, spoon into a casserole dish and top with the potato mixed with the onion. Bake at 180-190°C for about 30 minutes or until golden brown. Serves 4.

◆ EELS

Eels abound in our rivers but we, for the most part, ignore them as a food. Try them soused, like trout, and add a little cochineal to add a pink colour. This is more delicious than any tinned salmon could ever be.

◆ WHITEBAIT FRITTERS

1 tbsp flour
2 tbsp milk
2 eggs, well beaten

salt and pepper
2¼ cups whitebait

Make a batter of the flour, milk, eggs and seasonings. Add whitebait and fry in spoonfuls in hot oil or butter until lightly browned. Serve with lemon slices or wedges, mint sauce or apple sauce.

◆ WHITEBAIT SOUFFLÉ

2 tbsp butter
2 tbsp flour
1 cup milk
3 eggs, separated

1 cup whitebait
lemon juice
salt and pepper

First make a white sauce: Melt butter, stir in flour, add milk gradually stir until smooth. Add beaten egg yolks, then whitebait and flavourings. Fold in stiffly beaten egg whites. Place in fireproof dish and stand in pan of boiling water. Cook at 180°C for 30-35 minutes. Serve at once.

♦ WHITEBAIT IN CHEESE SAUCE

2 tbsp flour
2 tbsp butter
2 cups milk
1 cup grated cheese

parsley
salt and pepper
1 clove garlic
2 cups whitebait

To make sauce melt butter and add flour, stirring all the time. Add 1 cup milk gradually, stir until smooth. Then add the rest of the milk, grated cheese, flavourings and whitebait. Pour into greased ovenware dish, cover with breadcrumbs and dot with butter. Cook at 180°C for 30 minutes.

♦ SCALLOPS AND COCKLES

Scallops obtained in the shell are prepared by removing the flesh from the shells, then cutting off the heads and removing the black spots. Scallops may be eaten raw or used in the same way as mussels. Cockles are usually heated in water to remove them from their shells. Because they are small and not always available, they are more of a picnic-at-the-beach treat.

FISH SHELLFISH

♦ PIPIS

Pipis are usually opened by being heated in water. Place them in a frying pan with just sufficient water to prevent them sticking. As the shells open, remove the pipis and allow them to cook thoroughly. Shake a little pepper over them and add a nut of butter just before serving.

♦ WAYS WITH OYSTERS

Oysters minced make excellent sandwiches; minced and mixed with breadcrumbs and egg for a forcemeat stuffing for leg or shoulder of mutton; creamed for pies and patties; served raw on shell with lemon juice; added to steak for steak and oyster pie or pin bacon rasher round oyster, dip in egg and breadcrumbs, fry until golden brown.

♦ SCALLOPED OYSTERS

1½ dozen oysters
1½ cups breadcrumbs
¼ tsp salt

pepper
½ cup melted butter
⅓ cup full cream milk

Pick over oysters, removing pieces of shell. Mix breadcrumbs, salt, pepper and butter. Sprinkle one third of the breadcrumbs into a buttered baking dish. Add half the oysters. Then add another third of the breadcrumbs and remaining oysters. Add milk to oyster liquor, pour over oysters. Cover with remaining crumbs and bake at 200°C for 20-30 minutes or until done.

♦ CURRIED OYSTERS

1½ dozen oysters
4 tbsp butter
1 cup oyster liquid and milk

1½ tbsp flour
salt and pepper
¼ tsp curry powder

Sauté oysters gently in 2 tablespoons of the butter. Remove from heat and drain, reserving liquid. Add milk to make 1 cup. Melt remaining 2 tablespoons butter in saucepan, add flour and seasonings. Add liquid gradually and cook over low heat until thickened, stirring constantly. Add oysters and heat through. Serve with boiled rice. Serves 4.

♦ MOULES MARINIÈRES

50g butter
3 medium onions, diced
4 cloves crushed garlic, chopped
1 tsp black pepper
1 bay leaf

bunch chives, chopped
2 dozen fresh mussels in shells
½ glass dry/semi-dry white wine
1 large bunch parsley, finely chopped
125ml cream

Using a large pot melt butter gradually, and add onions and garlic to blanch. Add pepper, bay leaf, chives and mix well. When onion is soft turn stove to high, add mussels (which have been cleaned and beards pulled off) plus wine. Cover pot and shake vigorously many times or turn with large spoon. Add parsley and cream. Shake well. Put mussels (just cooked and still in shells) in a large dish. Reduce sauce a little and pour over mussels.

This recipe must be prepared quickly. Leftover sauce can be reused by adding half glass of water and half glass of wine. Makes an interesting entrée.

♦ FISH BRODERIE

6 hard-boiled eggs
6 tomatoes
125g butter
1 cup flour
1 x 425g can of cream of mushroom
  soup

3 cups milk
1 cup grated cheese
salt and pepper
¼ cup sherry *or* white wine
3 cups cooked fish, flaked

Slice eggs and tomatoes and arrange slices in neat rows over the bottom of a glass oven dish. In a saucepan melt butter and blend in flour. Stir in milk and cook, stirring until smooth and boiling. Stir in mushroom soup and half the grated cheese. Add seasonings, wine and fish. Turn into lined dish and sprinkle with rest of cheese. Bake at 180°C until tomato is cooked and the top light brown.

♦ SWEET AND SOUR FISH

500g boneless fish
1 egg
1 tbsp water

salt and pepper
$1/2$ cup cornflour
oil for frying

Sauce:

$1/2$ cup chopped onion
2 cloves garlic, crushed
1 tbsp oil
1 tsp gravy mix
$1/4$ tsp salt

$1/4$ tsp pepper
1 cup tomato purée
1 tsp brown sugar
$1/4$ tsp ginger
1 tbsp vinegar

Cut fish into approximately 4-cm squares. Beat together egg, water, and salt and pepper. Dip fish into egg mixture then roll in cornflour. Stand 10 minutes. Fry in oil until golden.

Sauce:

Sauté onion and garlic in oil. Stir in remaining ingredients, bring to the boil, simmer 5 minutes, and then pour over hot fish.

♦ SCRAMBLED FISH

1 cup cold cooked fish
3 tbsp milk
salt and pepper

2 eggs
chopped parsley
buttered toast

Put fish, milk and seasoning in pan and heat. Beat eggs and add to pan. Stir carefully until thick, then add parsley. Serve on buttered toast.

♦ FISH BALLS

50g bacon, chopped
2 tbsp butter
125g breadcrumbs
salt and pepper
2 tbsp milk
2 eggs, separated

225g cold fish
oil for frying
1 cup melted butter
anchovies
lemon juice

Fry bacon a pale colour in butter. Add breadcrumbs, seasoning, milk and egg yolks, and cook, stirring well. Add chopped fish and cook for a minute or two. Let this cool. Form into balls on a floured board. Fry in hot butter or oil. Drain on paper, then serve with melted butter sauce flavoured with anchovy and lemon juice. The sauce should be thick enough to cover the balls.

♦ FISH PIE

about 1 cup cold smoked fish, flaked
2 hard-boiled eggs
2 cups parsley sauce

breadcrumbs *or* mashed potato
peas and corn (optional)
butter

Grease pie dish and put in layers of fish, egg and sauce until dish is full. Corn and green peas may also be added. Cover with breadcrumbs or mashed potato. Place small pieces of butter on top and bake at 180°C until brown and crisp on top.

♦ FISH CAKES

1 cup mashed potato
450g cooked fish
$1/4$ tsp cayenne
salt to taste
1 tbsp butter
2 eggs

flour
1 cup white breadcrumbs
oil for frying
1 dsp chopped parsley
lemon wedges

Mix the potato, fish and seasonings together in a basin. Add melted butter and 1 egg (not beaten) to bind. Divide into cakes and roll in flour, beaten egg and finally breadcrumbs. Deep fry in hot oil for 5-8 minutes. Drain on paper before serving, garnished with parsley and lemon wedges.

♦ SALMON CASSEROLE

1 cup macaroni
450g salmon, flaked
50g butter
1 tbsp chopped onion
2 tbsp chopped pimento

$1/4$ cup flour
2 cups milk
salt and pepper
Worcester sauce
$1^1/2$ cup grated cheese

Cook macaroni in boiling salted water until tender. Drain and arrange in greased 2-litre casserole dish. Add flaked salmon and mix lightly. Melt butter and cook chopped onion and pimento until onion is golden. Blend in flour, gradually add milk and cook until sauce is smooth and thick. Add salt and pepper to taste and dash of Worcester sauce. Stir in grated cheese and pour this sauce over the salmon and macaroni. Bake at 180°C for 20 minutes.

♦ TUATUA FRITTERS

2 cups minced tuatuas
1 cup self-raising flour
1 egg

salt
small onion, chopped (optional)
milk

Mix all together with milk to a soft consistency and fry in hot oil.

◆ KEDGEREE

³/₄ cup raw rice
50g butter
225g smoked fish, cooked
2 hard-boiled eggs

salt and pepper
1 tsp chopped parsley
pinch of nutmeg
1 egg yolk

Boil rice until cooked and drain well. Add butter, fish and other ingredients to saucepan. Mix well together and heat gently until very hot.

Soups

SOUPS

◆ PUMPKIN SOUP FOR SLIMMERS

5 cups peeled and chopped pumpkin
500*ml* water
½ cup chopped onions
½ cup sliced celery
2 cloves garlic, crushed
1 chicken stock cube

¼ tsp ground fennel
¼ tsp ground ginger
pinch of black pepper
pinch of ground nutmeg
2 cups liquid skim milk
dill sprigs *or* chives to garnish

In large saucepan combine all ingredients except milk and bring to the boil. Reduce heat and let simmer about 20 minutes until pumpkin is tender, then cool a little. Pour 2 cups soup into blender or food processor and process until smooth. Transfer to large bowl and repeat with remaining soup, 2 cups at a time, until all processed. Pour soup back into pan, add milk and heat, stirring occasionally, until heated. *Do not boil.* Garnish with dill, or chopped chives. Serves 4.

◆ FISH SOUP

2 cups fish stock
1 onion, chopped
½ cup water
2 cups milk
2 tbsp chopped parsley

grated carrot *or* potato (optional)
1 packet cream of chicken soup
1-2 tbsp cornflour
water for mixing

Make fish stock by boiling backbones or heads for 20 minutes, then strain. Cook onion in water until soft. Add fish stock, milk and parsley. Bring to boil and add grated vegetables. Simmer 5 minutes. Thicken with chicken soup powder and cornflour mixed with a little water. Simmer 5 minutes more. Serve with croutons

◆ GAZPACHO

1 small onion, finely chopped
1 clove garlic, crushed
fresh herbs (parsley, chives, marjoram)
1 cup tomato purée
1 cup chicken stock
1 cucumber, peeled and diced
3-4 tomatoes, skinned, seeded
    and chopped

1 green capsicum, skinned, seeded
    and chopped
2 tbsp olive oil
2 tbsp white vinegar
dash tabasco
salt and pepper
croutons

Mix onion and garlic with finely chopped herbs and blend with purée and stock. Add cucumber, tomato and capsicum to purée, then oil, vinegar, tabasco and seasoning. Chill thoroughly and serve garnished with croutons.

♦ TOMATO SOUP

1 kg tomatoes, skinned and chopped
1 tbsp butter
1 onion, finely chopped
2 cups water
1 tsp green herb stock powder
$\frac{1}{2}$ tsp dried chervil

$\frac{1}{4}$ tsp basil (optional)
2 cups milk
2 tbsp cornflour
small amount of milk
chopped parsley to garnish

Place tomatoes, butter and onion in a saucepan. Simmer slowly, adding water when soft. Season with stock and herbs (optional). Simmer 10 minutes. Press through a sieve to get a pureé. Whilst simmering, heat the milk in another pan and thicken with cornflour blended with a little milk. When thickened add the cooked tomatoes slowly, stirring all the time. If too thick add more water. Add chopped parsley when serving.

♦ DELICIOUS TOMATO AND MUSSEL SOUP

2 packets tomato soup
1 medium onion, sliced
$3\frac{1}{2}$ cups milk

1 cup chopped mussels
2 crab sticks (optional)

Combine onion with soup mix and milk and cook. Cut up mussels and crab sticks and add to soup. Serves approximately 6. Reheating will improve flavour. Do not allow to boil after milk added.

♦ SEAFOOD CHOWDER

2 tbsp butter
2 onions, chopped
2 sticks celery, chopped
2 carrots, finely diced
2 potatoes, cubed
2 tsp green herb stock powder
2 tsp chicken stock powder

2 cups water
400-600g boneless fish
2 cups milk
chopped parsley
cornflour
water

Melt butter in a large pot, add onion, celery, and carrot. Cook 3 minutes without browning. Add potatoes, instant stock and water. Cover and simmer 5-10 minutes until vegetables are tender. Cube fish and add to vegetable mixture. Bring back to boil and stir in milk and parsley. Thicken with a little cornflour mixed with water.

◆ KUMARA CHOWDER

750g kumara, peeled
salted water
3½ cups milk
250g onions, chopped
4 celery sticks, chopped

25g butter
1 x 450g can creamed corn
salt and pepper
300ml cream

Boil kumara in salted water until tender. Drain and mash with milk. Sauté onion and celery in butter until soft, but not brown. Add to kumara. Mix with corn and bring slowly to the boil. Use a low heat as the mixture burns easily. If necessary add more milk, but the mixture should be rather thick. Season to taste. Stir in the cream and reheat but do not boil or the chowder may curdle. Garnish with parsley, crispy bacon or seafood.

To freeze: If desired, soup may be frozen before adding cream.

◆ SHELLFISH SOUP

500g paua, mussels *or* pipis
1 onion
1 tbsp butter

1 x 420g can coconut cream
salt and pepper

Mince shellfish and onion. Melt butter in a saucepan and sauté mixture lightly until cooked. Add coconut cream and seasoning, reheat and serve at once.

◆ PUMPKIN SOUP

1kg pumpkin, peeled and chopped
2 large onions, chopped
2 stalks celery, sliced
½ tsp salt
¼ tsp pepper

2-3 tsp sugar
milk
grated cheese and chopped parsley
    for garnish

Cook pumpkin, onion and celery in a little water until just tender. Purée in processor or blender. Add seasonings, sugar and reheat, adding sufficient milk to make required consistency. Reheat but do not boil. Serve sprinkled with cheese and parsley.

Poultry and
Game

♦ CHICKEN CHOP SUEY

spring onions
1 stalk celery
2 bamboo shoots
3 Jerusalem artichokes, fresh
   or canned
1 white cabbage heart
50g mushrooms
oil

2 cups chicken stock
1 dsp soy sauce
cold cooked chicken breastmeat,
   cut into strips
$\frac{1}{2}$ cup beansprouts
1 tsp butter
$1\frac{1}{2}$ tsp cornflour

Finely chop or slice vegetables (except beansprouts) and fry for 3 minutes in olive oil. Place in chicken stock with soy sauce. Bring to boil and cook gently for 5 minutes. Add beansprouts and chicken. Stir in butter squashed in cornflour and cook until thickened.

♦ CHICKEN CHOW MEIN

1 tbsp butter or oil
450g cold cooked chicken,
   cut in fine strips
1 onion
1 stalk celery, sliced finely

125g mushrooms, sliced finely
$\frac{1}{2}$ cup beansprouts
2 tsp soy sauce
1 tsp butter or oil
1 egg, beaten

Melt butter or oil and add half the chicken, tossing it in pan until slightly browned. Add onion, celery, mushrooms and beansprouts. Mix with 1 teaspoon soy sauce, cover and cook for about 10 minutes. Place this in the bowl you will serve it from and keep hot. Fry the rest of cut up chicken in a little butter or oil, add soy sauce and the beaten egg. Fry this in a small pan large enough to make a very thin chicken pancake. Turn this out on top of the chicken chow mein. Serve with crispy noodles. Chow mein can also be made with pork, crayfish, ham or veal.

♦ CHICKEN CASSEROLE

1 chicken *or* fowl
285*ml* cream
4 tbsp sherry

2 packets mushroom soup powder
1 tsp curry powder

Boil the chicken and take meat off the bones. Put all other ingredients into a saucepan, gradually bring to the boil and cook until thick. Tip sauce and chicken into a casserole dish and heat through in oven.

♦ DOUBLE L CHICKEN

30*ml* lemon juice	pinch of pepper
30*ml* lime juice	good pinch of ground ginger
1¹/₂ tsp lemon rind	1 clove garlic, finely chopped
1¹/₂ tsp lime rind	50*ml* water
2 tsp chopped parsley	chicken pieces

Combine lemon and lime juices, rinds, parsley and seasonings, and stir in water. Add chicken pieces and coat with marinade. Cover and refrigerate for at least 3 hours turning chicken several times. Bake at 200°C for 10 minutes. Reduce heat to 160°C and cook until tender approximately 35 minutes. Serve garnished with fruit. Serves 4.

♦ TURKISH CHICKEN

1 chicken *or* fowl	1 x 410g can tomatoes
water	salt and pepper
2 onions	225g rice
chopped fresh herbs	900*ml* chicken stock
6 peppercorns	¹/₂ cup blanched almonds
75g butter	

Boil chicken in water with one chopped onion, herbs and seasoning for 1¹/₂-2 hours. Cool and cut into pieces for serving. Slice the other onion, add to heated butter in pan and lightly brown. Pour tomatoes over, add salt and pepper and rice. Cook for 3 minutes, then add chicken stock and chicken joints. Continue cooking until the rice and chicken are tender, adding more stock if dry. Just before serving throw in chopped blanched almonds and serve immediately.

This dish is also very good made with rabbit.

♦ CHICKEN MARENGO

1 chicken, jointed	salt and pepper
¹/₂ cup olive oil	3 tomatoes, skinned and chopped
2 tbsp butter	2 tbsp sherry
50g bacon *or* ham	2 cups stock
1 onion, sliced	parsley and thyme
125g mushrooms, sliced	¹/₂ cup stuffed olives
2 tbsp flour	

Fry chicken joints in olive oil until brown and drain well. Melt butter, add chopped ham or bacon, sliced onion and mushrooms and cook for 5 minutes. Stir in flour, salt and pepper. Add tomatoes, sherry, stock, herbs and olives. Stir and simmer very gently for 30 minutes. Pour over chicken and cook at 180°C for 45 minutes.

♦ CREAMY CHICKEN AND MUSHROOMS

30g butter
50g mushrooms, sliced
6 spring onions, sliced
¼ cup sherry *or* port
2 x 435g cans cream of mushroom
    soup, undiluted

1½ cups milk
1 tsp Worcester sauce
¼ tsp cayenne
3 cooked chickens, cut into
    2.5 cm pieces
600*ml* sour cream

Heat butter in pan and add mushrooms and spring onions. Cook until mushrooms are soft. Add sherry or port, soup, milk, sauce and cayenne. Bring to boil, add chicken and sour cream, reduce to low heat. Cook until chicken is heated through.

♦ CHICKEN ON THE RUN

chicken pieces
salt and pepper
1 x 350g can apricots and juice

½ cup wine *or* water
1 packet mushroom *or* onion
    soup powder

Put chicken pieces into casserole dish. Sprinkle with salt and pepper. Pour in apricots and juice. Add wine or water, then sprinkle soup powder over. Let stand at least 15 minutes. Bake 190°C for 1 hour.

♦ ORIENTAL CHICKEN

½ cup flour
1 tsp ground ginger
1 tbsp chicken stock powder
1 x size 6 *or* 7 chicken, jointed
50g butter
4 small onions, quartered

1 clove garlic, crushed
1 packet thick vegetable soup
1 cup water
¼ cup dry sherry
1 x 450g can apricot halves

Combine flour, ginger and chicken stock in a paper bag, coat chicken pieces well, a few at a time. Heat butter in a pan and brown chicken pieces with onions and garlic. Mix soup powder with water and sherry. Put chicken and onions in casserole dish, add soup mixture. Drain apricots, reserve half the syrup and add to casserole. Cover and bake for 30 minutes at 180°C. Add apricot halves and continue cooking a further 30-45 minutes until chicken is tender. Serve with rice. Serves 5.

♦ ROAST WILD DUCK

Clean, wash and dry the dressed duck. Rub with lemon inside and out. Rub the skin with a clove of garlic sliced in two. Insert a stalk of celery and a small onion chopped in the cavity; add $1/2$ tsp of thyme and dust with salt and freshly ground black pepper. Tuck back the wings and truss. Dust the outside with salt and pepper. Place in a roasting pan with the back up. Cover with a thin slice of bacon or some ham fat. Add 1 cup of water to the pan and roast, breast side down, at 180°C allowing about 20-25 minutes per 450g depending on how well done is preferred. When half done, turn the breast side up. Baste frequently with the liquid in the pan. For really well done duck, roast until a leg pulls away from the bird when pulled with fingers. Serve with a tart jelly – crabapple or redcurrant – or with lemon and orange slices. Wild ducks are seldom stuffed. Serve with fluffy boiled rice, brussels sprouts and kumaras, with bananas and orange sauce.

♦ BRAISED WILD DUCK

Perhaps the best method for wild duck is braising. The risk of dry or tough meat is minimised. Take well cleaned ducks and brown slightly in a braising pan (heavy cast pan with lid or dutch oven). Season with salt and black pepper and add a pinch of rosemary, a diced onion, a stalk of celery, $1/2$ clove of garlic and $1/2$ cup of dry claret or burgundy. Cover and braise about an hour, basting frequently. Adding an apple while braising gives a favourable taste. Remove ducks from the stove. Make stock into light gravy and strain. Take thin outer layer of orange rind, cut into tiny thin strips and simmer in 2 tbsp of water and 1 tsp of sugar. Add to gravy with 2 tbsp of plum or currant jelly. Remove thighs and breast of cooked ducks and place in the sauce, simmering five minutes.

♦ JUGGED HARE

50g butter	parsley
1 hare, jointed	thyme
125g bacon	1 bay leaf
2 tbsp flour	2 onions
salt and pepper	6 cloves
300ml stock	2 tbsp butter
1 cup red wine	

Melt 50g butter in a pan and fry joints of hare until brown all over. Add cut up bacon and fry lightly.

Sprinkle in flour and let brown with the hare. Season to taste. Add stock, wine, herbs and one of the onions stuck with cloves. Cover and bake at 200°C for $1^1/2$ hours. Peel remaining onion and fry them in the 2 tbsp butter until well browned. About 15 minutes before the hare is ready add onions to the casserole. A few fried forcemeat (stuffing) balls make a nice addition, and redcurrant jelly should be served with it. For pressure cooking the time is 30 minutes.

♦ RABBIT PIE

1 rabbit, cut into small pieces
1 small onion stuck with cloves
1-2 lemon slices
salt and pepper
water *or* stock

6 slices ham *or* lean bacon cut into
  large pieces
3 hard-boiled eggs, cut into quarters
flour
short pastry

Place rabbit in a saucepan with onion, lemon, and salt and pepper. Almost cover with water or stock and stew until tender. Put rabbit in a pie dish with ham and hard-boiled eggs put on top. Discard onion and lemon, then thicken remaining liquid with flour to make gravy and pour over rabbit. Cover pie with short pastry and bake at 200°C for 20-30 minutes.

♦ GOOSE AU MADEIRA

Clean, wash and dry a dressed goose. Stuff it with apple halves lightly dusted with sugar, nutmeg and dipped in melted butter, prunes (8-12) which have been soaked in madeira for two days and some whole boiled chestnuts (may be canned). Roast at 180° oven, basting frequently with madeira, until the legs can be easily moved back and forth. Bake breast down then turn breast up and brown well. The skin should be crisp and the meat medium done. If you prefer a well done bird continue cooking and basting. Serve with a tart jelly.

POULTRY
GAME

♦ ROAST HAUNCH OF VENISON

1 venison roast
butter
salt and pepper

800g flour
water

Trim and wash meat, brush with melted butter, and sprinkle with salt and pepper. Mix together flour and water to make a stiff dough. Knead lightly. Roll out in to one piece big enough to cover roast. Roll round roast. Bake 170°C for 25-30 minutes per 500g for medium cooked, or 30-35 minutes per 500g for well done. When cooked, chip off paste and return meat to a very hot oven to brown. Serve with port-flavoured gravy and redcurrant jelly.

Meat

MEAT DISHES

♦ CREAMED HAM SAVOURY

1 tbsp butter
1 tbsp flour
1 cup milk
250g ham, minced

1 medium onion, minced or
  finely chopped
1/2 cup mashed potato
cooked pastry shell or flan case

Melt butter and add flour to make a roux, add milk and stir over heat until thickened. Combine with ham, onion and mashed potato, and fill pastry case. Serve hot or cold.

♦ SAVOURY SAVELOYS

3 large potatoes
1 onion
2 saveloys per person
30g cheese, grated

1 egg, beaten
salt and pepper
milk
4 strips bacon

Peel potatoes and place them in salted water to boil. Dice onion very finely. Part boil the saveloys, take the skins off. Split down centre, half way through. Drain potatoes and mash them. Add the onion, cheese, egg and pepper and salt. Mix ingredients completely, adding a little milk to cream the mixture. Spoon mixture into the split saveloys, wrap the slice of bacon around them. Place in oven dish and bake at 150°C for 20 minutes.

♦ LENTIL BURGUNDY

about 300g meat
4 medium onions, sliced
2 cloves garlic, crushed
3 medium carrots, sliced
6 tomatoes or 1/2 can tomato paste

500g lentils soaked for 24 hours
  in water
1 bay leaf
marjoram
sage

In a large saucepan sauté required meat (bacon bone or equivalent thick bacon pieces,chicken legs, cooking sausage or any leftover meat), and add onions, garlic and carrots. Then add soaked lentils and tomatoes or tomato paste, bay leaf, majoram and sage. Simmer for about 1 hour. This is a good winter's meal. Remember leftover lentils can be eaten cold as a salad.

MEAT

♦ VEAL AND CELERY

450g veal, cut in thin strips
cornflour
1 egg mixed with water
3 tbsp oil
1 onion, chopped
2 slices green ginger, chopped

1 large bunch celery, sliced
1½ tbsp soy sauce
½ cup water
2 tbsp cornflour
1 tbsp sugar
2 tbsp water

Dust slivers of veal in cornflour, stir into water and egg mixture. Heat oil very hot. Add onion, ginger and veal. Have heat very high. Stir-fry 5 minutes, then lift out. Heat oil again, add slices of celery and stir-fry for 5 minutes. Add veal and soy sauce. Toss contents round in pan about 4 minutes and add half a cup of water. Bring all to boil, leaving lid on and boil gently for about 3 minutes. Thicken with cornflour, sugar and 2 tbsp water mixed together. Cook 1 minute.

Pork, mutton or any meat can be used.

♦ SWEET AND SOUR PORK

1 tbsp cornflour
1 x 225g can pineapple pieces,
    juice drained and retained
140*ml* vinegar
¼ cup sugar
1 dsp Worcester sauce

½ tsp mixed mustard
1 x 330g can green beans, drained
salt and pepper
500g cooked pork cut into strips
1 green capsicum, cut into rings
1 red capsicum, cut into rings

Mix cornflour with some pineapple juice to a smooth paste, add vinegar and sugar, stir until thick and clear. Add Worcester sauce, mustard, green beans, and salt and pepper and simmer for 5 minutes. Add pineapple pieces and green and red capsicum rings and cook 2 minutes. Add pork and heat well.

♦ DRESSING UP MUTTON

For the housewife who finds lamb a little too expensive, here are some points on flavouring that will pep mutton up and make it a family favourite.

♦ A dash of vinegar or a few lemon slices in the water in which mutton is boiled will give piquancy. A basting of spiced vinegar, or vinegar in which herbs have been steeping, gives a new tang to a roast or a grill. Lemon juice or vinegar, or the sharp flavour of celery leaves, cress or caraway seeds, will sharpen the flavour of a casserole of mutton.

♦ Seasoned breadcrumb stuffing gives a savoury variety to a boned shoulder, breast or loin. Highly seasoned crumbs (you can use poultry seasoning) can coat the cutlets or chops to be baked in the oven.

♦ The brown sauces served with mutton should be well seasoned. Always serve a tart-flavoured accompaniment to roast mutton – mint sauce, tart jelly, spiced fruit or a well-flavoured onion gravy.

♦ CHOW MEIN

500g pork, chicken or skirt steak,
  finely sliced
oil for frying
Selection of sliced vegetables –
  courgette, cauliflower, celery,
  cabbage, carrot, spring onion
  or onion, beans, beansprouts,
  mushrooms

1 small can pineapple pieces
$\frac{1}{2}$ cup water
1 tbsp soy sauce
1 tbsp brown sugar
1 tsp cornflour
1 tbsp water

Marinade:

$\frac{1}{3}$ cup soy sauce
1-2 cloves garlic, finely chopped
salt and pepper

1 tbsp cooking oil
$\frac{1}{2}$ tsp finely chopped green ginger

Put sliced meat in marinade and leave to stand while preparing vegetables. Preheat frying pan with a little cooking oil and stir-fry meat until cooked. Transfer to bowl and keep warm. Add more oil to hot pan – put vegetables in and stir on a good heat. Cover for a few minutes. Add meat and some water to pan with soy sauce and brown sugar. Thicken slightly with cornflour mixed with water and adjust seasoning. To save time use a cooked chicken – flesh cut into bite size pieces. Also packets of frozen chow mein vegetables could be used instead of fresh. Serve with cooked rice.

♦ ROAST WING RIB OF BEEF

2kg wing rib of beef
butter *or* oil

$\frac{1}{4}$ cup claret *or* burgundy

Put meat in baking dish. Dot top with a little butter or oil. Pour in wine. Put in oven at 230°C for 15 minutes. Reduce to 200°C and cook, basting frequently for about 1$\frac{1}{4}$ hours or until cooked to preferred stage.

♦ SPANISH LEG OF LAMB

1 clove garlic
1 leg lamb
3 tbsp chopped mint
5 tbsp olive oil
2 tbsp lemon juice

1 tbsp tarragon vinegar
1 tbsp Worcester sauce
1 tsp salt
pepper
1 dsp sugar

Cut garlic into slivers and insert into lamb at intervals. Mix together remaining ingredients. Put meat into dish and pour mixture over. Bake at 250°C for 10 minutes, basting frequently. Reduce to 200°C and cook, basting until done. Thicken gravy in dish and strain before serving.

◆ STUFFED SHOULDER LAMB

1 rasher bacon
1 tsp butter
1 small onion, chopped finely
$\frac{1}{2}$ cup diced celery
$\frac{1}{3}$ cup canned crushed pineapple,
   juice retained

about $\frac{3}{4}$ cup breadcrumbs
1 tbsp chopped parsley
$\frac{1}{4}$ tsp ground ginger
salt and pepper
1 egg, beaten
1 lamb shoulder, boned

Fry bacon over low heat until softened. Remove from pan and chop. Add butter to fat in pan. Heat and then stir in onion and celery. Fry for 2 minutes. Add pineapple, breadcrumbs, bacon, parsley, ginger, salt and pepper. Fry for 2 minutes, remove to a bowl. Add the beaten egg and combine well. Sprinkle lamb with salt and pepper, spread with filling. Roll up and tie with string. Put into baking dish with a little butter or oil and bake at 180°C for 1$\frac{1}{2}$ hours. After meat has been in oven for 1 hour add about $\frac{1}{4}$ cup pineapple syrup to pan and baste occasionally.

◆ ROAST PORK WITH BARBECUE SAUCE

$\frac{3}{4}$ cup canned onion soup
$\frac{1}{2}$ cup water
$\frac{1}{4}$ cup vinegar
1 tbsp brown sugar
$\frac{1}{2}$ tsp salt

$\frac{1}{4}$ tsp pepper
1 dsp prepared mustard
1 thick slice of lemon
$\frac{1}{2}$ cup tomato sauce
1 pork loin

Combine onion soup, water, vinegar, sugar, salt, pepper, mustard and lemon slice. Simmer for 10 minutes and then stir in tomato sauce. Rub pork with salt and pepper. Place on rack in baking dish and bake in a hot oven 230°C for 10 minutes. Reduce to 180°C, add the sauce and cook basting frequently until tender. Strain the juice in the dish, skim and use to make gravy.

◆ HUNGARIAN PORK CHOPS

4 pork chops *or* pork leg, sliced
1$\frac{1}{2}$ cups white wine
2 carrots, sliced
1 onion, sliced
1 clove garlic
sprig of parsley

1 bay leaf
50g butter
a little flour
1 dsp paprika
breadcrumbs
salt and pepper

Marinate the meat in the wine, carrots, onion, garlic, parsley and bay leaf in a covered dish, turning over once, for 12 hours. Drain the meat, brown on both sides in the butter. Shake a little flour over, add a little of the strained marinade and simmer for 20 minutes. Sprinkle paprika over, add a little more marinade and continue cooking for 5 minutes. When the meat is almost done, place in a casserole with the vegetables, shake breadcrumbs and seasoning over and brown in oven at 220°C. Add more marinade if the chops dry up. Serve rest of marinade as sauce.

◆ MEXICAN PORK CHOPS

4 pork chops
1 onion, sliced
4 tbsp uncooked rice
1 x 425g can tomatoes or cooked
  fresh tomatoes

1 green capsicum
pinch of chilli powder
salt and pepper
chopped sage and thyme

Place chops and onion in a casserole with a spoonful of rice on each chop. Chop the pepper, mix with the tomato and chilli powder and pour over the rice. Sprinkle the salt and pepper and chopped herbs on top. Cover and bake at 180°C for 1 hour.

◆ DUTCH MEAT ROAST

1 thick slice of bread, crusts removed
1 cup hot milk
450g mince
2 rashers bacon, chopped
pepper

herbs
carrots, peas and onions (optional)
1 egg, beaten
1 cup gravy or stock

Place bread in basin and add milk. Cover and leave ½ hour. Add mince, bacon, vegetables, pepper and herbs to taste. Mix with egg, turn into a shallow baking dish and pour stock or gravy over. Bake at 180°C for 1 hour.

◆ ROAST PORK WITH APPLES AND SULTANAS

1 small joint pork
salt and pepper
½ cup water

4 medium apples
currants and sultanas

Dust pork with salt and pepper and place in baking dish. Add water. Core the apples and fill with currants and sultanas. Arrange apples around pork and bake at 180°C for 1½ hours.

◆ VEAL WITH GREEN CAPSICUM

675g veal steak, thinly sliced
seasoned flour
2 tbsp oil
2 cloves garlic, mashed
2 onions, sliced
225g mushrooms, sliced

salt and pepper
1 cup tomato purée
1 cup water
sprinkling dried basil
2 green capsicums, cut into strips

Toss veal in seasoned flour and fry quickly in oil over high heat. When browned reduce heat and add garlic, onions, mushrooms, salt and pepper. Cook, stirring constantly, 2 minutes. Add tomato purée, water, basil and capsicum. Cover and simmer 20-30 minutes or until veal is tender.

MEAT

♦ CORNISH PIE

Short pastry:

2 cups flour
125g butter *or* lard
1 tsp baking powder

$\frac{1}{2}$ tsp salt
$\frac{1}{2}$ cup milk

Filling:

225g minced meat
1 potato, finely chopped
1 onion, finely chopped
1 apple, finely chopped

1 tbsp parsley
salt and pepper
milk *or* egg for glazing

Make up pastry as usual and roll into two circles to fit a large ovenproof dish. Mix minced meat with vegetables, apples and parsley. Put one piece of pastry in the dish and cover with mixture. Add salt and pepper. Brush edges of pastry with milk or egg, then lay second piece on top. Brush top with milk or egg and bake at 200°C for 40 minutes.

♦ SHEPHERD'S PIE

1 medium onion, chopped fine
$\frac{1}{2}$ cup gravy
1 cup cooked minced meat
$\frac{1}{2}$ tsp salt
cold milk

$\frac{1}{4}$ cup hot milk
1 tbsp butter
1 cup mashed potatoes
pepper
chopped parsley

Mix onion with gravy, meat, salt and a little cold milk and put in casserole dish. Beat hot milk and butter into mashed potatoes, then add pepper and parsley. Cover meat with potatoes and bake at 180°C for 30 minutes. Serves 3.

♦ CORNED BEEF HASH

2 tbsp butter
1 cup chopped corned beef
3 cups chopped boiled potatoes

1 small onion, chopped
salt and pepper

Melt butter in frying pan. Combine other ingredients and spread mixture evenly over pan and brown slowly. When crust forms, turn as an omelette.

◆ CORNED BEEF À LA MODE

1 cup cooked corned beef
25g butter

1-2 tsp cornflour
1 cup milk

Remove fat from cooked meat, shred or dice meat. Fry gently in butter until well warmed through and slightly crisp. Sprinkle cornflour over mixture and stir well. Add milk gradually, stirring well until the right consistency is reached. Serve on toast.

Quantities may be varied to suit taste, and with more or less liquid as required.

◆ CASSEROLE FOR A CROWD

2 large onions, chopped
25g butter
1.5kg blade steak, cubed
3 tbs flour
1 x 400g can red kidney beans
1 cup cooked corned beef
1 x 400g can mushrooms

2 stock cubes
4 slices bacon, diced
$^1/_2$ cup tomato purée
$^1/_4$ tsp mixed herbs
salt and pepper
2 cups water

Sauté onions in butter. Toss cubed meat in flour. Mix all ingredients with water. Place in covered dish and bake about 2 hours at 180-190°C.

◆ MUTTON LEFTOVERS

2 cups cooked rice
2 onions, sliced
sliced cooked mutton
salt and pepper

parsley
$1^1/_4$ cups gravy *or* stock
breadcrumbs
butter

In a greased casserole dish put a layer of rice, layer of onions and layer of meat. Season and pour in a little gravy. Continue until casserole is full. Season and pour in gravy on each layer. Cover with breadcrumbs, dot with butter, brown in oven at 160°C for 40 minutes.

◆ SAVOURY MEAT ROLLS

$1^1/_2$ cups flour
pinch of salt
1 tsp baking powder
3 small potatoes, mashed
milk to mix

minced cold mutton
tomato sauce
parsley
oil for frying

Mix dry ingredients and potatoes with milk to a stiff dough and roll out to $^1/_2$ cm thick. Cover with mutton flavoured with tomato sauce and parsley. Roll up, cut into slices and fry in oil.

♦ CROQUETTES

1 tbsp butter
4 tbsp flour
1 cup milk
2 cups meat *or* vegetables for filling
1 tsp salt
pepper

1 tsp onion juice
1 egg beaten
breadcrumbs
salt and pepper
oil for frying

Croquettes are made from any left-over meats, fish, eggs, or vegetables such as mushrooms. The basic mixture for 2 cups of meat is:

Melt butter, stir in flour, then add milk a little at a time. Stir well and cook over low heat a few minutes to make a thick white sauce. Add meat or fish, minced or very finely chopped, salt, pepper and onion juice. Spread on a flat surface and cool. Roll into cylinders or cones, dip in egg, then seasoned breadcrumbs and fry lightly until well warmed through and crisp on outside.

♦ SAVOURY SAUSAGE PIE

flaky pastry
500g sausagemeat
1 medium apple, grated
1 medium onion, finely chopped
1½ cups cooked rice

2 tsp curry powder
1 egg, beaten
1 tsp salt
1 tbsp chopped parsley

Line sponge roll tin with pastry, reserving enough to make top. Mix other ingredients together and spread over pastry. Top with rest of pastry. Bake at 220°C for 30 minutes.

♦ ARGENTINE STEAK *(prepared overnight or early morning)*

1.25kg blade steak or lamb steaks
2 tbsp sugar
2 tbsp flour
1 tsp curry powder
1 tsp ground ginger
½ cup port

½ cup tomato juice
3 tbsp vinegar
1 tsp Worcester sauce
grated rind and juice of 1 lemon
2 bacon rashers, chopped
1 dozen prunes, stoned

Cut meat into pieces. Cover with sugar, flour, curry powder and ground ginger and rub in well. Place in casserole and pour over port, tomato sauce, vinegar, Worcester sauce, lemon juice and rind, chopped bacon and prunes. Leave to stand overnight or for some hours so that flavours will spread. Bake in covered casserole dish at 160-180°C for about 2 hours.

♦ CASSEROLES OF MEAT AND VEGETABLES

Casserole cooking has this great advantage for the busy housewife or the hostess – that all the preparation is done well ahead. The long, slow cooking of meats brings out the flavours and many delightful and varied mixtures may be tried out.

♦ HAMBURGER SPAGHETTI CASSEROLE

1 large onion, chopped
900g hamburger steak
butter for frying

450g spaghetti
2 x 425g cans tomato soup
salt and pepper

Brown onions and meat in butter. Cook spaghetti in 2.5 litre saucepan for 10 minutes or until tender. Drain and add to meat and tomato soup. Season, turn into casserole and bake at 180°C for 1 hour.

♦ LAMB HASH CASSEROLE

1/3 cup chopped onion
1 tbsp butter
1 cup cold diced potatoes
2 cups cubed cold roast lamb
1 cup leftover gravy

1/3 cup tomato soup
water
salt and pepper
grated cheese *or* breadcrumbs
butter

Brown onion lightly in butter then put in casserole dish with other ingredients except last two. Sprinkle with grated cheese or breadcrumbs and dot with butter. Cook at 180°C for 20 minutes or until browned.

♦ SWEDISH MEATBALLS

1/2 cup breadcrumbs
2 cups milk
2 egg yolks
1/2 cup chopped onion
butter for frying
450g chuck steak, minced

125g pork, minced
225g veal, minced
salt and pepper
1/2 tsp ground ginger
flour for thickening

Soak breadcrumbs in milk and egg yolk. Sauté onion in butter, add to meat, season and mix all ingredients together thoroughly, usingf sufficient flour to stiffen mixture. Chill in refrigerator 4 hours. Shape into tiny meatballs. Fry in butter until brown.

MEAT

◆ MEATBALLS IN SAUCE

Meatballs:

450g sausagemeat
1 onion, grated
³/₄ cup fine dried breadcrumbs
1 egg
½ cup milk

salt and pepper
flour
1 tsp chopped fresh herbs
2 tbsp oil for frying

Sauce:

1 tbsp butter
1 onion, grated
1 tbsp chopped green capsicum
1 tbsp chilli sauce
½ cup tomato sauce

½ tsp dry mustard
1 tsp prepared horseradish
1 tsp Worcester sauce
sprinkling tabasco sauce
chopped olives

Meatballs:

Mix sausagemeat, onion, herbs and breadcrumbs. Beat egg, add milk, salt and pepper, add to meat, mixing in herbs thoroughly. Make into small balls using a little flour. Heat oil, sauté meatballs until cooked.

Sauce:

Melt butter, fry onion and pepper about 5 minutes without browning. Add remainder of ingredients. Reheat and serve with meatballs.

◆ SWEET AND SOUR MEATBALLS (1)

Meatballs:

1.25kg mince
2 eggs
2 cloves garlic
salt and pepper

½-1 cup breadcrumbs
1 cup flour
oil for frying

Sauce:

1 cup sugar
9 tbsp soy sauce
1½ cups water
3 tomatoes, cut in wedges

9 tbsp vinegar
4 tbsp cornflour
3 green capsicums, sliced
1x 225g can pineapple pieces

Meatballs:

Mix together meat, eggs, garlic, seasonings and breadcrumbs with a little of the flour. Roll into balls and toss in rest of flour. Fry in oil until brown.

Sauce:

Place all ingredients in a saucepan and heat, stirring, until thickened. Place meatballs in baking dish, cover with sauce and cook until heated through.

♦ SWEET AND SOUR MEATBALLS (2)

Meatballs:

500g mincemeat	$^1/_4$ cup flour
1 cup breadcrumbs	2 tbsp oil
$^1/_4$ cup chopped parsley	juice from 1 x 440g can pineapple
salt and pepper	pieces
1 egg	1$^1/_4$ cups chicken stock
1 onion	

Sauce:

2 tbsp cornflour	4 tbsp vinegar
4 tbsp brown sugar	reserved pineapple pieces from can
2 tbsp soy sauce	

Meatballs:
Combine mince and breadcrumbs, parsley, salt, pepper and egg. Peel and finely chop onion, stir into meat mix. Form into 4-cm balls. Toss in flour. Heat oil in heavy base saucepan, add balls and brown evenly. Drain off excess oil. Cover the meatballs with pineapple juice and stock. Simmer 20-30 minutes. Cool slightly.

Sauce:
Mix together cornflour, brown sugar, soy sauce and vinegar. Stir into mince balls and bring to boil. Simmer 3-4 minutes, add pineapple pieces and heat through. Serves 4.

♦ DANISH MEATBALLS

450g veal, finely minced	1 egg
125g pork, finely minced	salt and pepper
1 tbsp flour	butter
150*ml* milk	

Mix meat with flour, milk and beaten egg. Season. Make into flat cakes and fry in butter. Serve with cauliflower, creamed spinach, mashed swede or turnips, with plenty of butter and pepper.

MEAT

♦ BARBECUING

As an alternative to the usual steaks and sausages on your barbecue, try kebabs – meat, fruit and vegetable chunks broiled on skewers and served with tangy sauces. Provide plenty of soaked wooden barbecue sticks, metal skewers or twisted wire skewers. Bricks at either end of the grill on the top of the barbecue will act as racks for the filled kebabs. Choose tender, fast cooking foods for the best kebabs. Before loading up the skewers, run them through a piece of fat so the food will push off easily when the grilling is done. Suggestions for kebabs include:

♦ sliced saveloy wrapped in bacon, pickled cucumber slices, cooked potatoes
♦ marinated lamb, tiny tomatoes, onion slices
♦ cubes of ham, orange sections, partially cooked onions
♦ cubes of bacon, onion, sausage slices
♦ cubes of ham, pineapple chunks, olives
♦ cubes of chicken wrapped in bacon, tiny new potatoes, partially cooked onions
♦ marinated beef, cucumber slices, olives.

♦ BARBECUE GRILLING ON FOIL

For barbecued hamburgers, cook them on foil. Tear off a strip the size of the griller top. With a skewer make small holes at 5 cm intervals to allow the heat to come up and the fat to go down into the fire. Turn up a 1 cm edge on the foil and place the hamburger patties on it when it's hot. Grill onion rings alongside. Serve the patties in toasted buns with slices of tomato and cucumber generously topped with barbecue sauce.

Bacon and **ham** will brown and crisp perfectly on foil. Grill pineapple rings as well alongside the meat.

Potatoes cooked in foil are the right partners for barbecued meats – chicken, steaks and chops. Scrub medium-sized potatoes (or yams or kumaras) and brush with butter or salad oil. Wrap each one in foil and cook for 45-60 minutes either in the embers or on the griller. Turn the vegetables occasionally.

Sweet corn is delicious cooked either on foil or on the grill. Leave the corn wrapped in its leaves and turn occasionally.

♦ MARINATED PINEAPPLE STEAK

1kg rump steak	$^1/_2$ tsp pepper
$^1/_2$ cup pineapple juice	2 tbsp oil
$^1/_2$ cup lemon juice	$^1/_4$ tsp dry mustard
2 tsp soy sauce	$^1/_2$ tsp salt

Cut steak into serving slices and place in marinade made by combining remaining ingredients. Cover and refrigerate overnight. Remove from marinade and pat dry. Place on barbecue and cook quickly. Serve with tossed salad. Serves 6-8.

♦ BARBECUE SKEWERED LAMB CUTLETS

Marinade:

1½ tbsp Worcester sauce
1 tbsp chilli sauce
1 tsp salt
1 onion, grated
2 cloves garlic, crushed

1 cup oil
½ cup vinegar
freshly ground black pepper
1 tbsp rosemary leaves

Kebabs:

8 large lamb cutlets
8 small tomatoes
8 small button onions
1 large sweet potato

1 green capsicum
2 lemons
8 large mushroom caps
8 bay leaves

Combine all marinade ingredients and mix well. Place cutlets in marinade. Chill tomatoes. Parboil onions for about 8 minutes. Peel sweet potato, cut into 1-cm thick slices, parboil for 10 minutes. Wash capsicum, cut into eighths lengthwise and remove seeds. Add to cutlet marinade and marinate for 3 hours. Slice lemons into 8. Wipe mushrooms and brush with melted butter. Thread meat, vegetables and tomatoes on to 8 skewers with the lemon slices and bay leaves. Barbecue over glowing coals for about 10 minutes, turning and occasionally brushing meat with remaining marinade.

♦ TO SERVE WITH YOUR BARBECUE

cauliflower
broccoli

spring onions
onion and chive dressing

Cut cauliflower and broccoli into small florets and blanch. When cool add finely chopped spring onions. Pour over enough onion and chive dressing to coat. Delicious with barbecued meat.

♦ IRISH STEW

Place the chops, cutlets or a forequarter of mutton (which should be cut into neat pieces, and seasoned with salt and pepper) around the sides of a saucepan. Place them so that the pieces lie loosely on top of one another until the saucepan is nearly full. In the empty space in the centre put raw medium-sized onions, a little raw celery and medium-sized raw potatoes. Fill the saucepan, not quite covering all with lukewarm water, place on stove and cover with a lid, bringing to the boil. Keep the saucepan to one side and simmer steadily for one hour. Then leave the saucepan where it will keep hot on the stove but will not cook any more and leave for half an hour when the fat can be skimmed off and the stew served with some chopped parsley.

MEAT

♦ FRENCH IRISH STEW

This paradoxical title developed from an Irishman trying to explain to a French restaurateur how to make Irish Stew. This was the result and is so good the recipe is a firm favourite. Meat cooked this way hardly shrinks at all and is much improved in flavour.

6 medium potatoes, peeled and
   thickly sliced
2 onions, sliced
1 clove garlic

salt and pepper
1 x 675g joint of lamb
25g butter
1 cup stock

Put potatoes, onions and garlic in a baking dish. Salt and pepper well then place the joint, also well seasoned, on top of the vegetables and dot with butter. Pour stock over and bake at 160°C for 1-1½ hours.

♦ BEEF STEW

675g stewing beef, cut in 2-cm cubes
1-2 kidneys, quartered
1 large onion, cut into pieces
1 carrot, cut into pieces

¼ cup flour
1 tsp salt
1 cup water

Sprinkle meat and vegetables with flour and place in a casserole dish, pressure cooker or pot. Add salt and water. If the stew is in a casserole, cook it in a slow oven at about 160°C for 3 hours. If in a pot, leave simmering slowly but not boiling for about the same time. In a pressure cooker, the stew should be cooked for 20 minutes and potatoes can be cooked in with it by placing whole large potatoes on top of the meat and vegetables.

♦ HARICOT STEW

6 leg *or* neck mutton chops
¼ cup seasoned flour
fat
1 large carrot, sliced
1 medium onion, chopped
1 swede, chopped

1 turnip, chopped
75g haricot beans
salt and pepper
2 cups stock *or* water
¼ cup flour
cold water

Trim fat from chops. Dip them in seasoned flour, brown in a little fat and put in saucepan. Add vegetables, beans, seasoning and stock and simmer stew for about 3 hours. Thicken shortly before it is served with flour mixed to a smooth paste with a little cold water.

◆ CURRIES

Curries are a tasty nutritious alternative to the usual menu. Curry powder must be cooked after it has been worked into the dish; the longer the cooking the better the flavour. The flavour of curry is much enhanced by the inclusion of a clove of garlic and by the use of tomato juice, or diluted tomato purée. Curry pastes can be used instead of powder. Make your curry well ahead of time, in the morning of the day it is to be served, or even the day before. It will improve in flavour by standing.

Condiments are served separately in small bowls to accompany curry:
◆ Salted peanuts
◆ Green or red capsicums cut into small slices
◆ Shredded coconut, grated carrot and sultanas, mixed
◆ Sliced mushrooms fried in butter and flavoured with garlic
◆ Sliced cucumber, garlic, salt and yoghurt
◆ Mango chutney
◆ Pineapple cubes
◆ Tomato slices, chopped red onion, sugar, salt, sweet chilli sauce, vinegar
◆ Finely sliced hard-boiled eggs
◆ Slices of banana
◆ Preserved ginger and other various imported condiments.
◆ Poppadoms and rice

◆ CURRY SAUCE FOR ANY SAVOURY

1 onion, sliced
25g butter, melted
1 tbsp curry powder *or* to taste
425*ml* milk
1 dsp chutney
1 dsp sultanas

1 dsp sugar
1 dsp coconut
salt and pepper
1½ tbsp flour
10*ml* milk

Sauté onion in melted butter with curry powder. Add 425g milk, chutney, sultanas, sugar, coconut, and salt and pepper to taste. When almost boiling, thicken with flour which has been mixed to a paste with 10*ml* milk. Simmer three minutes.

To this can be added many things, depending on the cook's ingenuity:
◆ Chopped crayfish meat, parsley and lemon juice
◆ Cold fish, chopped or flaked
◆ Oysters
◆ Mushrooms
◆ Hard-boiled eggs, halved or quartered
◆ Cooked, diced vegetables

♦ CURRY

2 cups stock
2 level dsp dessicated coconut
750g cooked meat *or* 350g fresh meat
   (lamb, beef, veal)
1-2 dsp curry powder
oil
1 onion

75g flour
1 dsp chutney
1 small apple
1 dsp sultanas
1 tsp salt
1 tbsp lemon juice

Bring stock to boil, pour over coconut and infuse. Cut meat into cubes and dip in curry powder. Fry meat lightly and remove. Fry onion, then add flour and rest of curry powder and cook for a minute. Drain stock from coconut. Add stock, chutney, chopped apple, sultanas and salt and bring to boil. Add meat and simmer 1-1½ hours. Add lemon juice and serve with boiled rice. (See Page XXX for correct method of cooking rice.)

♦ VEGETABLE CURRY

1 apple, diced
1 onion, diced
1 tbsp curry powder
25b butter
3 tbsp flour
1½ cups stock *or* vegetable water

salt
1 tbsp tomato chutney
900g mixed raw root vegetables, diced
125g beans, diced
juice of ½ a lemon

Fry apple, onion and curry powder in butter for 15 minutes without burning. Add flour and cook well, then some stock or vegetable water, salt and tomato chutney. Add vegetables to sauce, bring to the boil and turn into a casserole. Cook at 160°C in oven until the vegetables are tender – about 1½ hours. Before serving add lemon juice.

♦ INDIAN CURRY

900g lean meat
butter *or* oil
1 tbsp curry powder
stock
2 onions
1 apple
2 carrots

other vegetables of choice
½ cup sultanas
1 dsp brown sugar *or* golden syrup
1 dsp ground ginger
salt and pepper
1 tsp vinegar

Dice meat and fry in a little butter or oil until brown. Add curry powder and fry a little longer then place in saucepan and cover with stock. Bring to boil and simmer for two hours. Dice and fry vegetables until light brown. Add them with other ingredients to meat and cook half an hour. Serve on rice.

◆ COLD MEAT PATTIES

350g flaky pastry
125g cooked meat, minced
25g breadcrumbs

salt and pepper
stock *or* gravy to moisten
1 beaten egg *or* milk

Roll out pastry thin and cut to line patty tins. Mix all ingredients except milk. Place a little mixture in each patty tin, moisten edges with milk and cover with pastry. Press and flake edges and brush with egg or milk. Make a small hole in centre of each pattie. Bake at 230°C for 10 minutes.

◆ CONTINENTAL MEATLOAF

350g steak, minced
oil or butter for frying
220*ml* tomato purée
125g egg noodles
2 tbsp milk soured with lemon juice

$1/2$ cup cottage cheese
1 tbsp chopped onion
$1/2$ small green capsicum, chopped
2 tbsp melted butter
salt and pepper

Place minced steak in frying pan with heated oil or butter and fry until brown. Add tomato purée, mix well, remove from heat. Cook noodles, place in bottom of greased ovenware dish, keeping about one-third for border. Combine milk, cheese, onion and capsicum and spoon on top of noodles. Top with meat and tomato mixture and season. Stir melted butter through remaining noodles and arrange in a border. Bake at 180-200°C for 30 minutes. Serves 4.

◆ MEATLOAF

900g beef, minced
225g veal *or* sausagemeat
2 eggs, beaten
1 cup breadcrumbs

1 cup milk
1 onion, minced
salt and pepper
tomato sauce to taste

Mix all ingredients well together. Press into loaf pan. Cover with foil or greased paper. Cook at 180°C for 1 hour. This mixture may be made into small balls or flat cakes and baked or fried.

MEAT

♦ HAM AND BEEF LOAF FOR PICNICS

675kg beef, minced
350g ham *or* bacon, minced
2 cups soft breadcrumbs
salt to taste
2 eggs, beaten
1½ cups milk

½ cup brown sugar
½ tsp dry mustard
¼ tsp ground cloves
¼ tsp nutmeg
¼ tsp cinnamon

Mix meats, breadcrumbs and salt together. Beat egg and milk and stir in thoroughly. Mix sugar and spices together and spread over bottom of well-greased loaf tin. Press loaf mixture into tin. Cover with well-greased foil or buttered paper. Bake at 180°C for 1½ hours.

♦ LAMB LOAF

675g mutton *or* lamb, minced
1 onion, minced
½ clove garlic, finely chopped
1 x 425g can tomato soup
2 eggs, well beaten
1½ tsp salt

¼ tsp pepper
½ cup cream
900g boiled mashed potatoes
salt and pepper
3 tbsp butter

Grease loaf tin. Mix first seven ingredients together. Place in tin and bake at 180°C for 1½ hours. Beat potatoes with butter, cream and seasoning until light and fluffy. Turn loaf out of tin on to baking dish or ovenproof dish. Spread mashed potatoes all over loaf and brush with melted butter. Place in oven again at 180°C for 15 minutes or until lightly browned. Garnish with brightly coloured vegetables.

Many variations of meat loaves may be made by altering the mixture of meats and adding or removing various flavourings. In recipes using mince and sausagemeat, increasing the amount of sausagemeat and decreasing the amount of mince will make a smoother texture.

♦ Try minced veal with some chopped oysters, as the base for a loaf
♦ Use some of the condensed soup flavours, mushroom, tomato, asparagus, to give variety in flavour
♦ Use rice, macaroni or oatmeal instead of breadcrumbs
♦ Make small individual loaves or shapes

♦ MEXICAN MEATLOAF *(very tasty and pungent)*

675g steak, minced
125g veal, minced
125g pork, minced
2 eggs, beaten
1¼ tsp salt

1 tbsp parsley
2 onions, minced
1 green capsicum, chopped
2 red capsicums, chopped
small onions, parboiled

Topping:
melted butter

breadcrumbs

Mix all ingredients, except onions, together well and form a loaf shape to fit your casserole, leaving a little room all round. Brush all over with melted butter, sprinkle with breadcrumbs. Place small parboiled onions around the loaf and cook 1 hour at 180-200°C. Serve in the casserole.

Desserts

♦ PATRIOTIC PARFAIT

Alternate layers of fresh blueberries, raspberries and natural yoghurt in tall glasses, finishing with yoghurt. Decorate with a blueberry or raspberry on top. If too tart add liquid sweetener to yoghurt. Serve immediately.

♦ BRANDY BASKETS

60g butter
3 tbsp castor sugar
2 tbsp golden syrup
4¹/₂ tbsp flour

¹/₂ tsp ground ginger
¹/₂ tsp mixed spice
1 tsp brandy *or* finely grated lemon peel
oiled apple *or* orange (to shape biscuits)

Combine butter, castor sugar and golden syrup in a saucepan. Stir over a slow heat until melted. Sift in flour and spices, add lemon peel or brandy and beat until glossy. Heat oven to 180°C. Line trays with non-stick paper. Spoon a teaspoon of mixture leaving room to spread. Put only 4 or 5 on a tray. Bake one tray at a time until golden brown (6-7 minutes). Cool until slightly set. Quickly lift each biscuit, bubbly side up, on to oiled orange or apple. Flute into a cup with fingertips. Cool on rack. Fill with whipped cream and fruit. Biscuits keep in airtight tin.

♦ COFFEE RICE

1 tsp instant coffee
¹/₄ tsp salt
¹/₂ cup rice
1¹/₂ cups boiling water
¹/₂ cup seedless raisins,
    washed and drained

140*ml* cream
2 tbsp sugar
dash vanilla
¹/₄ cup chopped nuts
1 tbsp drained cherries
    (maraschino *or* canned)

Put coffee, rice and salt in boiling water. Cover and cook over low heat for about 20 minutes. Add raisins, cover and cook a few minutes longer until raisins are plump. Cool thoroughly. Whip cream with sugar and vanilla until thick. Fold into cooled rice with nuts and cherries.

♦ BUTTERSCOTCH SPONGE JELLY

2 eggs, separated
2 cups hot milk
25g butter
1 cup brown sugar

2 dsp gelatine
¼ cups hot water
whipped cream

Whisk egg yolks with hot milk and cook slowly until thickened. Cool. Melt butter and add brown sugar and stir into cooled custard. Dissolve gelatine in hot water and add to custard mixture. Beat egg whites until very stiff and fold lightly through. Set in wetted mould until firm, turn out and decorate with whipped cream.

♦ PINEAPPLE CLOUD

1 x 450g can pineapple cubes
1 packet pineapple jelly
1 cup boiling water

1 egg, separated
140*ml* cream
small meringue halves

Drain pineapple and divide fruit out into tall-stemmed glasses. Make up pineapple jelly with boiling water. Add pineapple juice and water (if needed) to make up to 2 cups in all. Allow to cool to setting point. Whisk egg white. Whisk yolk until foamy and fold the two together. Spoon over fruit in the glasses. Top with a little whipped cream and a small meringue half.

♦ CARAMEL SAUCE

6 tbsp sugar
3 tbsp water

5 tbsp water

Dissolve sugar in first measure of water. Bring to boil and heat until golden brown. Remove from heat and add carefully second measure of water. Stir until water is well mixed in and leave to cool. Use as required. This sauce will keep for several weeks.

♦ BAKED ALASKA

1 sponge cake, 2.5 cm thick
fruit juice
port *or* sherry

ice cream
4 egg whites
6 tbsp sugar

Just moisten spongecake with fruit juice and port or sherry. Place on ovenproof plate. Freeze a block of ice cream very hard. Whip egg whites until stiff and fold in sugar. Place ice cream on top of sponge cake and cover thickly with meringue, completely sealing ice cream and cake. Bake at 230°C for 4-5 minutes to lightly colour meringue. Serve at once.

◆ HEAVENLY PIE

Shell:

1 cup sugar	4 eggs, separated
¼ tsp cream of tartar	

Filling:

½ cup sugar	⅛ tsp salt
3 tbsp lemon juice	575*ml* cream
1 tbsp finely grated lemon rind	

Shell:

Sift sugar and cream of tartar. Beat egg whites until stiff but not dry, gradually add sugar mixture, beating until thoroughly blended. Use this meringue to line bottom and sides of a well-greased pie plate hollowing out the centre and being careful not to spread meringue too close to the rim. Bake at 140°C for one hour, then cool.

Filling:

Beat yolks slightly. Stir in sugar, lemon juice, rind and salt, and cook in double boiler until very thick (about 8-10 minutes). Remove and cool. Whip cream and combine half of it with lemon-egg mix and fill meringue shell. Cover with remaining whipped cream. Chill in refrigerator about 24 hours. Serves 6-8.

◆ PARFAIT FLUFFY COCONUT PEARS

1 egg white	2 tbsp sugar
1 dsp lemon juice	½ cup dessicated coconut
¼ tsp grated lemon rind	4 canned pear halves, well drained
1 tbsp pear syrup	

Combine egg white, lemon juice and rind, syrup and sugar in heatproof basin. Place over saucepan of boiling water and beat 4-5 minutes with beater or until mixture stands in peaks. Remove from heat and add coconut. Pile on to pear halves.

◆ APRICOT WHIP

dried apricots	1 tsp lemon juice
water	pinch of salt
⅓ cup sugar	2 egg whites, stiffly beaten

Cook dried apricots in very little water, sweeten them slightly. Drain off juice and purée the fruit. To each cupful of purée add the measured sugar, lemon juice, salt and beaten egg whites. Stir egg whites well into mixture and serve chilled.

♦ KNICKERBOCKER GLORY

sweetened raspberry purée
1 measure strawberry ice cream
sliced peaches

whipped cream
1 raspberry, strawberry *or*
  maraschino cherry

Place a layer of sweetened raspberry purée in a tall glass. Add, in order, a scoop of strawberry ice cream and a layer of sliced peaches (or other fruit). Add more raspberry purée to flow down through glass and another scoop of ice cream. Top with whipped cream and a raspberry, strawberry or maraschino cherry.

♦ LEMON CHIFFON SQUARE

Crust:
115g butter,
  melted

1 packet wine, malt *or* ginger biscuits,
  crushed

Filling:
1 tbsp gelatine
$^1/_2$ cup water
2 eggs, separated

juice and rind of 1 lemon
$^1/_2$ cup sugar

Crust:
Mix melted butter and crushed biscuits together and press into a tin. Chill.

Filling:
Dissolve gelatine in water and heat slightly. Drop in egg yolks and mix until well blended, then add lemon juice and rind. Beat egg whites, add sugar and beat again. Fold into first mixture. Pour into crust. Cool in refrigerator. Decorate with whipped cream and chocolate, if liked.

1 packet jelly
boiling water
fresh apples, strawberries and
  bananas, sliced

2 dsp condensed milk
whipped cream (optional)

Make up jelly as directed on the packet and before it sets, divide into two bowls. To one bowl add sliced fresh fruit and leave to set. To the other bowl add condensed milk and beat until frothy. Pour the beaten mixture over the fruit jelly and leave to completely set. Whipped cream may be spread on top if desired.

♦ THE OLD BREAD PUDDING

6-8 slices bread
$^1/_4$ cup sugar

2 large eggs
600*ml* milk

Leave crusts on the bread and dampen under the tap. Squeeze out water and break up the bread, add sugar and eggs and beat with a fork. Add milk and blend well. Bake at 180°C for 1 hour or until set.

Variations – add raisins, spread with jam when set, cinnamon *or* nutmeg sprinkled over top before cooking. A very good way to use up stale bread.

♦ JELLIED CHRISTMAS PUDDING

45g gelatine
60*ml* boiling water
15g cocoa
285*ml* milk
¹/₂ cup mixed peel
¹/₂ cup raisins
¹/₂ cup sultanas

60g sugar
425*ml* black coffee
1 tsp vanilla
few drops almond essence
¹/₂ cup cherries
15*ml* sherry

Soften gelatine in boiling water. Blend cocoa with milk and bring to boil. Add peel, raisins, sultanas and sugar. Simmer 5 minutes. Cool then add coffee, vanilla, almond essence, gelatine, cherries and sherry. Pour into wetted mould to set. Turn out and decorate with sprigs of holly.

♦ EASY TRIFLE

1 trifle sponge
1 x 400g can peaches, fruit salad
    or other fruit
1 raspberry instant pudding

milk
300*ml* cream, whipped
chocolate hail

Cut sponge into glass bowl. Chop fruit and pour over sponge. Make up instant pudding with milk according to packet directions and pour immediately on to fruit. Set aside for a few minutes until pudding firms up then spread with whipped cream. Sprinkle with chocolate hail.

♦ AMERICAN LEMON CHEESE CAKE

Crust:

2 cups sweet biscuit crumbs

125g butter, melted

Filling:

1 packet lemon jelly crystals
³/₄ cup boiling water
¹/₄ cup lemon juice
1 dsp grated lemon rind
1 x 375g can evaporated milk, chilled

250g cream cheese
1 cup castor sugar
1 tsp vanilla
whipped cream

Crust:

Combine biscuit crumbs and melted butter. Press on to bottom and sides of buttered 23cm spring- form tin. Bake at 180°C for 10 minutes. Cool and chill.

Filling:

Dissolve jelly crystals in boiling water, add lemon juice and rind, cool slightly. Beat evaporated milk until thick. In another bowl beat cream cheese until smooth and blend in sugar, vanilla essence and the beaten evaporated milk. Fold in warm jelly mixture. Pour into prepared crust and chill several hours or overnight. Decorate with whipped cream.

121

♦ BANANA CREAM

2 eggs, separated
575ml milk
1½ tbsp sugar
1½ tbsp gelatine

2 tbsp water
½ cup cream
3 bananas

Beat the egg yolks. Add milk and sugar and heat, stirring. Cool a little. Add gelatine already swollen in water. Let cool. Then add stiffly beaten egg whites, beaten cream and sliced bananas. Chill until firm.

♦ BANANA WHIP

4-5 bananas
1 tsp vanilla
1 cup sugar
1½ tbsp gelatine

2½ cups boiling water
2 dsp cocoa
cream

Mash bananas with vanilla and sugar. Dissolve gelatine in ½ cup hot water. Add 2 cups boiling water in which cocoa has been dissolved. Add bananas, leave to set. Serve with cream.

♦ CALEBS DELIGHT

1 packet orange *or* pineapple jelly
½ cup hot water

1 cup fruit salad
300ml ice cream

Put all ingredients in a pot. Stir until ice cream is melted. Pour into bowl and leave to set. Can be decorated with whipped cream and chocolate chips.

Variations:
Boysenberry jelly and canned boysenberries
Pineapple jelly and crushed pineapple
Fresh fruit may also be used

♦ COFFEE MOUSSE (1)

1 tbsp instant coffee
3 tbsp sugar
1½ tbsp gelatine

285ml boiling water
285ml cream

Mix coffee, sugar and gelatine. Pour on boiling water. Stir until melted, then cool. Beat cream and stir in. Pour into bowl to set.

◆ GOOSEBERRY FOOL

gooseberries
sugar
vanilla custard

vanilla essence
cream

Rinse and top and tail some gooseberries. Stew them in a little water. Then rub through a sieve and sweeten to taste. When cold, mix with half their quantity in custard and half in flavoured whipped cream. Serve in tall glasses. Decorate each on top with whipped cream and serve with sponge fingers.

◆ FRUIT FLUMMERY

1 tbsp flour
cold water
1/2 cup fruit juice
juice of 1/2 lemon
3 tbsp sugar

1 cup hot water
2 tbsp gelatine
1/4 cup hot water
fresh *or* canned fruit

Mix flour to a smooth paste with a little cold water. Add fruit and lemon juices and sugar to the 1 cup of hot water. Carefully add the flour and boil for five minutes. Add gelatine dissolved in 1/4 cup hot water. Mix well and leave to cool. Then whisk until thick and foamy. Add any chopped fruit available and pour into a bowl to set.

◆ APRICOT FLUFF

2 cups stewed *or* preserved apricots
1/2 cup icing sugar

1/2 cup cream, whipped
1/2 cup dessicated coconut

Rub apricots through sieve. Add sugar. Fold in cream and most of coconut. Sprinkle a little coconut on top and serve cold.

◆ APPLE TRIFLE

450g apples
juice and grated rind of 1 lemon
1 cup sugar
small amount of water

2 egg whites
575*ml* custard
whipped cream

Pare, core and slice apples and stew with grated lemon rind and juice. Add sugar and very little water. Beat whites of eggs stiffly and mix lightly with the apples. Pile high on a dish and top with custard and a little whipped cream.

♦ JELLY RICE DESSERT

1 cup rice
1 packet pineapple jelly
hot water

300*ml* cream, whipped
1 x 250g can crushed pineapple

Boil rice and cool. Make up jelly as usual and, when nearly set, add cold cooked rice, whipped cream and pineapple. Set in fridge. Also good with raspberry or blackberry jelly and fruit.

♦ COFFEE MOUSSE (2)

4 tbsp hot water
10g (1 sachet) gelatine
2 level tbsp instant coffee

4 heaped tbsp castor sugar
1 large can evaporated milk,
  chilled 2-3 hours

Measure hot water into basin and add gelatine, stirring until dissolved. Stir in coffee and sugar. Whisk evaporated milk until thick. Gradually whisk in coffee and sugar mixture. Leave to set in fridge. Decorate with whipped cream and chopped nuts or grated chocolate. (This is beautiful.)

♦ LEMON SNOW

$1/2$ cup sugar
2 cups warm water
2 tbsp cornflour

2 tbsp cold water
juice of 1 lemon
2 egg whites

Bring sugar and water to boil. Mix cornflour and cold water, add and bring to boil. Then set aside to cool and add lemon juice. Beat the whites of eggs stiff. Then beat into sugar mixture until white and foamy. Chill and serve with fruit and cream.

♦ MARSHMALLOW SHAPE

1 tbsp gelatine
$3/4$ cup hot water *or* fruit juice
3 eggs, separated

$3/4$ cup sugar
1 x 225g crushed pineapple,
  juice drained

Put gelatine and hot water on heat to melt. In a large basin place unbeaten whites of eggs, sugar, and add the gelatine and water. Beat all together until thick and set. Mix in pineapple. Put aside to cool and set. Make custard with yolks of eggs and when cool spread on top of marshmallow shape.

◆ PINEAPPLE PAVLOVA ROLL

4 egg whites
1 tsp cornflour
2 tsp vinegar
8 tbsp sugar

toasted coconut *or* slivered almonds
225g can crushed pineapple, drained
300*ml* cream, whipped

Whip egg whites, add cornflour and beat slightly. Add vinegar, still beating. Add 6 tablespoons of the sugar, and beat until stiff and glossy. Fold in last 2 tablespoons of sugar. Spread mixture evenly into greased and lined sponge roll tin. Sprinkle with coconut or almonds. Cook at 160°C for 15 minutes or until golden brown. Tip pavlova on to sugar-sprinkled baking paper and gently peel off greased paper. Cool slightly, spoon on pineapple and spread with whipped cream. Roll up from long side and chill in fridge overnight or at least 2 hours. Flaked chocolate can also be used as a filling.

◆ UNCOOKED PIE CRUST

50g sugar
225g wine biscuits, crushed

125g butter, melted

Mix sugar and biscuit crumbs. Pour in melted butter. Blend well. Press firmly over bottom and sides of pie plate. Chill well.

◆ PINEAPPLE CREAM

2 tsp gelatine
1 x 225g can pineapple pieces
  in juice
1 cup juice (make up with water)

2 eggs, separated
$1/4$ cup sugar
vanilla to taste
whipped cream

Soak gelatine in juice. Heat slowly until dissolved. Beat egg yolks and sugar until thick. Add gelatine and juice and vanilla. Fold in stiffly beaten whites. Pour over pineapple pieces. Chill. Decorate with whipped cream.

◆ RICE DESSERT

$1/3$ cup rice
2 cups milk
sugar

1 x 450g can crushed pineapple, drained
1 cup cream, whipped
grated chocolate

Boil rice in milk until thick. Add sugar to taste. When cool add pineapple. Add cream and decorate with grated chocolate or as desired.

♦ PAVLOVA

4 egg whites
pinch of salt
1½ cups sugar

¼ tsp baking powder
1 tsp vinegar
2 tsp cornflour

Beat egg whites and salt until stiff and fluffy. Add other ingredients and beat on low until very stiff. Pile on to greased foil on baking tray. Bake at 110°C for approximately 1½ hours. If starts to brown before this turn oven off. You may also cook in oven after roast. Turn oven off and leave overnight.

♦ PAVLOVA BASKETS

3 eggs, separated
1 cup sugar
vanilla essence

1 tsp vinegar
2 tsp cornflour

Filling:
1 cup milk
1 tbsp butter
1 x 225g can crushed pineapple

custard powder
whipped cream

Beat egg whites until stiff. Add sugar, essence and vinegar and fold in cornflour. Make small baskets on oil with forcing bag. Cook at 120°C until set. Make custard with egg yolks, milk and butter and custard powder. Fold in pineapple and fill baskets. Decorate with whipped cream.

♦ BOYSENBERRY CREAM

300*ml* cream, whipped
1 packet marshmallows, chopped

1 x 425g can boysenberries, drained

Mix all ingredients together, put in small dishes or one large bowl. Use liquid from fruit to drizzle over top. Chill and serve.

♦ RHUBARB DELIGHT

1 red jelly
1 cup boiling water
1 cup milk

2 cups cooked rhubarb
whipped cream

Melt jelly in water. Cool, then add milk. Stir well. Add rhubarb, fold in. Set in fridge. Decorate with whipped cream.

♦ FEATHER PUDDING

1 egg
1/2 cup sugar
1 tbsp melted butter
1/2 tsp soda

1/2 cup milk
1 cup flour
1 tsp cream of tartar
3 tbsp jam

Beat egg and sugar and add butter. Dissolve soda in milk and add to mixture. Then add sifted flour and cream of tartar. Place jam in greased pudding basin and cover with pudding batter. Cover securely with foil. Boil in saucepan of water for 1 hour. Turn out to serve.

♦ FRUIT CRISP PUDDING

1 jar fruit *or* mixed fruit
3 bananas
4 tbsp fruit syrup

50g butter
75g brown sugar
2 cups crushed cornflakes

Cut up fruit and add sliced bananas. Add fruit syrup. Place in flameproof serving dish. Melt butter and add sugar and cornflakes. Spread over fruit. Grill until crisp and brown on top.

♦ APPLE CRISP PUDDING

4 apples, peeled and cored
3/4 cup water
cinnamon

2 1/2 tbsp butter
3/4 cup white *or* wholemeal flour
1/2 cup raw sugar

Slice apples into pie dish. Pour over cold water and sprinkle with cinnamon. Rub butter into flour and sugar until crumbly. Put on top of apples and bake at 180°C for 30-45 minutes. No sugar is required in apples as it soaks through from the crust. Bake at 190°C for about 30 minutes or until fruit is soft and top crisp.

♦ BAKED ROLY POLY

1 cup flour
1 tsp cream of tartar
1/2 tsp baking soda

pinch of salt
125g butter
water to mix

Syrup:
1/2 cup sugar
1 tbsp butter

1 cup boiling water

Sift flour, cream of tartar, baking soda and salt. Rub in butter and mix to a firm dough with water. Roll out, spread with syrup. Roll up, seal ends and place in buttered dish. Dissolve sugar and butter with boiling water to make syrup. Pour over roly poly and bake at 190°C for about 45 minutes.

◆ GOOSEBERRY UPSIDE-DOWN CAKE

4 tbsp butter
1 cup brown sugar
450g gooseberries, topped and tailed
1 egg
1 cup sugar
2 tbsp softened butter

1 cup flour
1 tsp baking powder
1 tsp cinnamon
$^1/_2$ tsp salt
$^1/_4$ cup milk

Melt first amount of butter and mix with brown sugar. Spread on bottom of square tin and add gooseberries. Beat egg and sugar, add softened butter and beat well. Sift dry ingredients and add alternately with milk. Pour over fruit in tin. Bake at 180°C for 30-40 minutes. Serve hot with whipped cream.

◆ HOT CHOCOLATE SOUFFLÉ

2 tbsp butter
1 tbsp flour
1 tbsp cocoa

2 tbsp sugar
$^1/_2$ cup milk
3 eggs, separated

Melt butter, stir in flour, cocoa and sugar. Cook gently. Add milk slowly and stir until thick. Remove from heat and add beaten egg yolks. Beat well and cool. Fold in stiffy beaten egg whites. Pour into buttered dish and bake at 180°C for 30 minutes. Serve immediately.

◆ CHOCOLATE PUDDING

50g butter
2 tbsp sugar
2 eggs, separated
3 tbsp flour

$^1/_4$ tsp salt
1 tbsp cocoa
1 small tsp baking powder

Cream butter and sugar and add yolks of eggs. Add the dry ingredients and then beaten egg whites. Cook in a greased pie dish at 190°C for 15 minutes. Serve with custard and stewed fruit.

◆ VELVET CHOCOLATE PARFAIT

1 tbsp butter
1 tbsp golden syrup
$^1/_3$ cup brown sugar
75g dark cooking chocolate

2 eggs, separated
125*ml* milk
250*ml* cream, whipped
1 tsp vanilla essence

Heat gently together butter, golden syrup, brown sugar and chocolate. Remove from heat. Beat egg yolks into the melted mixture. Add milk and beat again for 1 minute. Beat the egg whites to a stiff froth and stir into the mixture. Add cream and vanilla and mix well. Pour into freezing trays and freeze until firm, stirring once.

♦ DESSERT CRÊPES

½ cup flour
¼ tsp salt
½ tsp sugar

3 eggs, separated
¾ cup milk
lemon juice, jam *or* sweet sauce

Sift flour with salt and add sugar. Beat yolks of eggs and mix with milk. Pour this liquid gradually into flour, stirring briskly. Beat egg whites until they will stand in peaks, then fold into batter. Rub frying pan with butter, heat and test with a little of the batter. If it burns immediately, cool pan down a little before starting to cook pancakes. Pour in enough of the batter to make a pancake about 17 cm across. When bubbling on top, turn over and cook on other side until pale gold. Serve either rolled up or flat with lemon juice, sugar, jam, or a sweet, liqueur-flavoured sauce.

♦ DELICIOUS APPLE PUDDING

1 cup flour
1 tsp baking powder
50g butter
about ⅓ cup of milk
apples *or* other fruit, chopped

cloves (optional)
1 cup hot water
1 tbsp butter
1 tbsp sugar

Make a scone dough of flour, baking powder, butter and milk. Roll out flat and place apples sprinkled with sugar and a few cloves. Roll up, and place in a buttered pie dish. Dissolve butter and sugar in hot water and pour over the roll. Bake at 200°C for 45 minutes. Any fruit can be used instead of apples.

♦ FROSTED APPLES

apples
melted butter
sugar
coconut
chopped dates
raisins

nuts
1 cup boiling water
1 cup sugar
coconut to garnish
cream

Peel and core apples. Roll each apple in melted butter and afterwards in sugar, then in coconut. Put in baking dish and fill centres with chopped dates, raisins and nuts. Mix boiling water with sugar and pour around apples. Bake at 160°C about 45 minutes until tender. Sprinkle with coconut and serve with cream.

◆ DATE PUDDING

75g butter
1/2 cup sugar
2-3 eggs
3 tbsp milk

125g stoned dates, finely chopped
1 tsp lemon juice
1 1/2 cups flour
1 tsp baking powder

Beat butter and sugar to a cream. Add eggs and beat well. Then add milk, dates and lemon juice. Sift in flour and baking powder. Steam 2 hours in a buttered mould.

◆ LEMON CHIFFON PIE

Biscuit crust:
1 cup crushed wine biscuits
60g butter, melted

1/4 cup brown sugar
1/2 tsp cinnamon

Filling:
1 tbsp gelatine
1/4 cup cold water
4 eggs
1 cup sugar

1/2 cup lemon juice
1 tsp salt
1 tsp lemon rind

Biscuit crust:
Mix biscuit crumbs with melted butter, brown sugar and cinnamon. Line a flan dish, pressing the mixture in firmly. Chill.

Filling:
Soak gelatine 5 minutes in the water. Separate eggs and add half cup sugar, lemon juice and salt to beaten egg yolks. Cook in a double boiler until thick. Add softened gelatine to custard mixture and stir until dissolved. Add rind and cool. Beat egg whites. Add second 1/2 cup of sugar and continue beating. Fold into custard and spoon into biscuit crust.

◆ LEMON PUDDING

1/2 cup sugar
2 tbsp flour
1 tbsp butter

juice of 1 lemon
2 eggs, separated
1 cup milk

Mix sugar, flour, butter and lemon juice together. Add well-beaten egg yolks and milk. Stiffly beat egg whites and add to mixture. Pour into pie dish. Stand in dish of hot water and bake at 180°C for about 30-40 minutes.

♦ MACARONI STEAMED FRUIT PUDDING

75g macaroni

sugar

fresh, stewed *or* canned fruit

Well cook macaroni in boiling water. Strain off, reserve liquid and line a small pudding bowl with the macaroni. Fill with any fruit – fresh, stewed or tinned – adding sugar to taste and enough macaroni stock to moisten. Place more macaroni on top and cover with greased paper. Steam 30 minutes and serve with a sweet sauce.

♦ PINEAPPLE PIE

1 x 225g can of pineapple pieces

3 tbsp sugar

2 egg yolks

1 tbsp cornflour (more if needed)

2 cups milk

Meringue

2 egg whites

$1/4$ tsp cream of tartar

$1/2$ cup sugar

Drain juice from pineapple into saucepan and reserve pineapple pieces. Add egg yolks, milk, sugar and cornflour and cook, stirring until thick. Turn into a pie dish. Top with pineapple pieces.

Meringue:
Beat all ingredients together until stiff. Spoon over top of pie. Bake at 190°C for about 15 minutes.

♦ PUMPKIN PIE

pastry

$1^{1}/_{2}$ cups milk

$^{3}/_{4}$ cup brown sugar

$1/2$ tsp ginger

$1/2$ tsp salt

$1/2$ tsp cinnamon

$1^{1}/_{2}$ cups cooked, mashed pumpkin

2 eggs, beaten

Line a flan dish with rolled out pastry. Mix all filling ingredients together and spoon on to pastry base. Bake about 200°C for 20 minutes then lower temperature to 180°C and cook a further 30-40 minutes or until filling is set.

♦ MUM'S CARROT PUDDING

$1^{1}/_{2}$ cups flour

1 cup raisins

1 cup suet

1 cup currants

1 cup grated carrot

1 tsp baking soda

1 cup grated potato

1 tbsp hot water

1 cup sugar

Mix first 7 ingredients together well. Add soda dissolved in hot water. Pour into greased bowl and steam 3 hours. This pudding is an excellent Christmas pudding.

♦ SINBAD PUDDING

1 egg
1/2 cup sugar
juice of 1 small lemon
1 cup flour
1 tsp baking powder
1/2 tsp salt

1/2 tsp mixed spice
1/2 tsp cinnamon
50g butter
1/2 cup brown sugar
a little milk

Beat egg, sugar and lemon juice together until thick. Put in greased pudding bowl. Sift flour, baking powder, salt and spice. Rub in butter. Add brown sugar. Mix with milk to make a moist dough. Spoon on to lemon mixture but do not mix. Steam for 1 hour.

♦ SPONGE CRUST FOR FRUIT

2 eggs
3/4 cup sugar
4 tbsp flour

1 tsp baking powder
boiled fruit

Beat eggs and sugar until thick. Fold in flour and baking powder. Put fruit in pie dish and heat in oven until syrup is boiling. Spread sponge mixture over. Bake at 200°C for about 20 minutes.

♦ BANANA ROLLS

1 cup flour
50g butter
pinch of salt

1 tsp baking powder
about 1/3 cup milk
banana

Syrup:
50g butter
1/2 cup sugar

1 cup boiling water

Rub butter into sifted flour, salt and baking powder. Mix with enough milk to make a stiff dough. Roll out and cut into squares. In each square place 1/3 of a banana (or 1/2 according to size), and make into parcels which are then placed standing up in a deep pie dish.

Make syrup by boiling butter, sugar and water. Pour around dish and bake at 180°C for 30 minutes.

◆ BANANA FRITTERS

2 cups self-raising flour
1/2 tsp baking soda
1 1/2 cups water
4 bananas

small amount of flour
oil for deep frying
ice cream

Sift measured flour and baking soda into bowl and add water. Mix to a smooth batter. Peel bananas, cut into three and roll lightly in flour. Drop banana pieces into batter. Drain off excess batter. Deep-fry in hot oil until golden brown. Remove, drain on paper towel and serve hot with ice cream.

◆ KIWIFRUIT AND APPLE AMBER

4 cooking apples
4 tbsp sugar
2 tbsp butter
1 tbsp lemon rind
2 tbsp lemon juice

2 eggs, separated
6 kiwifruit
4 tbsp castor sugar
1 tbsp chopped nuts

Peel, core and slice apples. Tip into a saucepan with the sugar, butter, lemon rind and juice. Cover and cook gently until apples are tender. Add egg yolks to apple, beat with a fork or whisk until well mixed. Peel and slice kiwifruit. Arrange the apple and kiwifruit slices in layers in an ovenproof dish. Place into a cold oven and cook as the oven heats to 160°C. Beat egg whites until stiff peaks form. Fold in castor sugar and pile meringue on top of apple mixture. Sprinkle chopped nuts over the meringue and bake until just brown.

◆ LIME SELF-SAUCING PUDDING

30g butter
1/2 cup castor sugar
2 eggs, separated
2 tbsp self-raising flour

1 tsp finely grated lime rind
125*ml* lime juice
200*ml* milk

Cream butter and sugar until creamy, add egg yolks and beat well with electric mixer. Stir in sifted flour, lime rind, juice and milk and mix well. Beat egg whites until soft peaks form, gently folding into the mixture. Pour into a lightly greased 6 cup capacity ovenproof dish. Bake at 160°C for 45 minutes. Dust with icing sugar and serve immediately.

♦ RHUBARB CREAM TART

400g prepared pastry
1 egg
$^1/_2$ cup sugar
2 tbsp flour

2 cups finely chopped rhubarb
juice and grated rind of 1 lemon
butter

Line a dish (approx 22 x 20 cm) with uncooked pastry. Beat egg, add sugar, and flour. Mix in rhubarb and rind and juice of lemon. Put mixture into pastry and dot with butter. Cook at 230°C for 12 minutes, then lower heat to 180°C for 20-25 minutes.

♦ STEAMED FRUIT PUDDING *(Very nice as a Christmas pudding)*

2 cups flour
1 cup sugar
1 cup sultanas
1 cup currants
50g peel
$^1/_2$ tsp mixed spice

$^1/_2$ tsp nutmeg
$^1/_2$ tsp cinnamon
60g butter
1 cup boiling water
2 tsp baking soda
1 cup cold water

Mix all ingredients except last 4. Mix butter and boiling water, then dissolve baking soda in cold water. Pour both mixtures into fruit and mix well. Put mixture into pudding steamer lined with lunch wrap – *don't put lid on*. Leave overnight. Cover steamer with lunch wrap before putting lid on. Steam 4 hours. This pudding can be made taken out of steamer and stored in the freezer. (If doing this, return to steamer from freezer, reheat for 2 hours). Serve with your choice of sauce, custard, whipped cream or ice cream.

♦ TAMARILLO STRUDEL

6 tamarillos
$^1/_2$ cup chopped walnuts
$^1/_4$ cup sugar
1 tsp cinnamon
1 tsp lemon rind

50g butter
1 cup soft breadcrumbs
375g puff pastry
50g butter, melted
icing sugar

Skin tamarillos and chop into 2 cm pieces. In a bowl mix together walnuts, sugar, cinnamon and lemon rind. Melt first measure of butter and mix into breadcrumbs. Roll out pastry to 35 x 55-cm rectangle. Melt second measure of butter and brush over pastry, leaving 5-cm margin all around. Arrange tamarillos along long edge of pastry. Sprinkle on walnut mixture. Fold in 2 short ends and roll pastry from long side. Place on greased oven slide. Brush with melted butter. Bake 30-35 minutes at 200 °C. Brush with butter once during cooking. Sprinkle with icing sugar and serve warm. Serves 5-6.

♦ TAPIOCA CREAM

1 cup tapioca
600*ml* boiling milk
3 eggs, separated
3 tbsp sugar

1¹/₂ tbsp coconut
6 tbsp sugar
coconut to garnish

Soak tapioca overnight in cold water. Drain off water and stir tapioca into 600*ml* boiling milk and cook 10 minutes. Beat the egg yolks with first amount of sugar and coconut. Stir into the boiling milk and tapioca and cook 5 minutes. Pour into greased pie dish. Top with meringue made from egg whites stiffly beaten with second amount of sugar and sprinkle with coconut. Bake at 180°C to brown the meringue.

♦ ICE CREAM (1)

2 tsp gelatine
1 cup hot water
1 cup castor sugar

325*ml* milk
500*ml* cream, whipped
1 tsp vanilla

Dissolve gelatine in hot water. Mix with castor sugar and milk, place in refrigerator tray in refrigerator for 30 minutes, then remove. Whip cream with vanilla. In a bowl mix cream with set gelatine and beat with an egg beater for a few minutes. Turn out into freezer tray and freeze until half set. Mix with fork then freeze hard.

♦ ICE CREAM (2)

1 x 440g can sweetened
   condensed milk
800g fresh milk
1 tbsp gelatine

125*ml* boiling water
1 x 400g can unsweetened
   condensed milk

Mix together first two ingredients. Dissolve gelatine in boiling water. Beat gelatine mixture and unsweetened milk together and half freeze. Combine with first mixture and beat well. Half freeze, then beat again and freeze.

♦ ICE CREAM (3)

2 eggs, separated
¹/₂ cup sugar

300*ml* cream, whipped
flavouring to taste

Beat egg whites with half the measure of sugar. Beat yolks with remainder of sugar. Fold all together with cream and flavouring, and freeze.

♦ ICE CREAM (4)

1 *litre* milk
1 can sweetened condensed milk

1 cup cream
pinch of salt

Place all ingredients in a bowl and whip. Place in freezer. When frozen around the edges, whip until fluffy, place in freezer trays, and return to freezer to set.

♦ BANANA ICE CREAM

3 large bananas
2 tbsp lemon juice
1 cup icing sugar

2 egg whites, beaten
1 cup cream, whipped
chopped nuts

Mash bananas with lemon juice and icing sugar. Add egg whites, whipped cream and chopped nuts. Freeze.

♦ AVOCADO ICE CREAM (*pale green and delicious*)

2 ripe avocados
juice of 2 lemons
3 eggs, separated
3 tbsp honey

1 tsp vanilla
1½ cups whipped cream
walnuts and peaches to garnish

Mash avocado flesh with lemon juice. Stir egg yolks, honey and vanilla over low heat until creamy. Cool. Beat egg white until stiff. Fold avocado mixture, egg custard, egg whites and whipped cream together. Cover and freeze. Serve decorated with walnuts and peaches.

♦ STRAWBERRY ICE CREAM

½ cup sugar
½ cup water
4 egg yolks

1½ cups cream
2 cups strawberry purée

Dissolve sugar in water and boil until a little when tested forms a thread. Pour hot syrup on to the yolks, beat until thick and light. Stir in the lightly whipped cream, fold in strawberry purée. Freeze in a covered container.

♦ CITRUS ICE CREAM

1 can unsweetened condensed milk
¾ cup sugar
2 oranges

2 bananas
2 lemons

Chill the condensed milk overnight. Whip the milk until thick and creamy. Add the sugar gradually, and beat well. Beat in the juice of the oranges. Mash the bananas with the juice of the lemons, fold into mixture. Pour into a large mould or freezer trays. Freeze until firm.

♦ ICE CREAM CAKE

Cut square sponge cake into pieces suitable for individual servings. The cake may be previously iced. Pile high with ice cream and top with whipped cream and nuts. Freeze until served.

♦ ICE CREAM WITH HOT CHOCOLATE SAUCE

1 can sweetened condensed milk
1 cup water

2 cups cream, lightly whipped

Sauce:
2 tbsp cocoa
1/2 cup boiling water
1 tbsp butter

1 cups sugar
2 tbsp golden syrup
vanilla essence

Mix condensed milk with water and add whipped cream. Half freeze, then beat, return to freezer.

Sauce:
Mix cocoa with hot water and bring to the boil with butter. Add sugar and syrup, boil for about a minute, add vanilla and serve hot, with ice cream.

♦ PINEAPPLE CHIP ICE CREAM

1 can unsweetened condensed milk
1 x 225g can crushed pineapple
2 tsp gelatine

1/4 cup sugar
55g chocolate

Chill condensed milk then beat until thick. Drain the pineapple, and soak the gelatine in 2 tablespoons of the juice. Dissolve the gelatine over hot water, add remaining juice and dissolve the sugar. Cool and mix into the milk. Stir in the pineapple pieces and the grated chocolate. Freeze in trays for an hour, stir well then refreeze.

♦ LAYERED ICE CREAM LOAF

2 *litres* vanilla ice cream
30*ml* coffee liqueur *or* milk shake flavour
15*ml* lemon juice
2 cups mixed dried fruit (cherries, sultanas, apricots, etc.)

2 egg yolks
2 tbsp sugar
1/2 cup chopped toasted almonds
  or chocolate chips

Divide ice-cream into three and keep frozen. Mix coffee liqueur into one third of the ice cream and spread into the bottom of a lined 20 cm loaf tin and return to freezer. Mix lemon juice and fruits into second portion of ice-cream and spread on top of coffee layer. Beat the egg yolks and sugar until creamy, add almonds or chocolate chips and mix into the last third of ice cream and freeze. Turn on to a serving plate and return to freezer until required.

Sauces,
Seasonings,
Stuffings and
Marinades

SAUCES, SEASONINGS, STUFFINGS AND MARINADES

♦ BARBECUE SAUCE

1 cup tomato sauce
1/2 cup water
1/4 cup golden syrup
1 tsp salt

2 tsp Worcester sauce
1/2 tsp dry mustard
1/4 tsp pepper
1 clove garlic, crushed

Mix well and let stand to mellow a few hours. Use to baste meat on griller or spoon on to hamburgers or hot dogs while cooking.

♦ APPLE SAUCE

2 tbsp whole cloves
2 tbsp whole allspice
4kg apples, minced
4kg sugar

1/4 cup salt
6 large onions, minced
1/2 tbsp cayenne
2.25 *litres* vinegar

Tie whole spices in a bag. Boil with all ingredients in a large saucepan for 3-4 hours. Discard whole spices. Bottle and seal. Keeps well.

♦ PLUM SAUCE

3kg plums
125g garlic
1kg sugar
1.75 *litres* vinegar
6 tsp salt

2 tsp cayenne
2 tsp ground cloves
2 tsp ground ginger
2 tsp ground pepper
a few blades of mace

Boil all ingredients together in a saucepan until mixture reduced to a pulp. Stir frequently. Force as much as possible through a sieve. Bottle when hot and seal.

♦ TOMATO SAUCE

5.5kg ripe tomatoes,chopped
1 cup cold water
2.77kg apples, minced
4 onions, chopped
1.75kg sugar
75g salt

2.25 *litres* vinegar
1 tbsp cayenne
2 tbsp black peppercorns
2 tbsp whole allspice
2 tbsp whole cloves

Boil tomatoes in the water one hour. Strain and add all the other ingredients with whole spices tied in muslin and boil 3-4 hours. Discard whole spices. Press through a sieve and bottle.

♦ MINT SAUCE

1 cup sugar
1 cup water

2 cups vinegar
1 cup chopped mint

Boil sugar, water and vinegar together and pour over mint. Bottle when cool.

♦ HORSERADISH SAUCE

1 can sweetened condensed milk
½ cup vinegar

salt and pepper
¾-1 cup grated *or* liquidised horseradish

Mix all ingredients together. This freezes well in small containers. Especially good with beef sausages.

♦ MUSTARD CORNED BEEF SAUCE

50g butter
2 eggs beaten
3 tablespoons sugar
2 tablespoons mustard

1 cup vinegar
liquor from meat to get correct
    consistency

Heat all ingredients together in a saucepan. Stir well while simmering until as thick as honey. *Do not boil.*

♦ BREAD STUFFING

1½ tbsp onion
¼ cup celery
3 tbsp melted butter
½ tsp salt

pepper
½ tsp thyme
2 cups breadcrumbs

Mix together all ingredients thoroughly.

♦ SAUSAGE STUFFING

225g pork sausages
½ cup breadcrumbs
chopped parsley to taste
chopped thyme to taste
1 clove garlic, crushed

2 tbsp melted butter
1 rasher bacon, chopped
salt and pepper
1 egg, beaten

Mix together all ingredients thoroughly.

♦ MUSHROOM STUFFING

Use above recipe, replacing sausages with mushrooms.

♦ STUFFING FOR CHICKEN

4 tbsp butter, melted
2 cloves garlic, crushed
2 medium onions, chopped
225g veal and saugage meat, minced

1 tsp salt
freshly ground black pepper
2 eggs, beaten
$\frac{1}{2}$ cup brandy (optional)

Mix all ingredients together to get an even mixture.

♦ MARINADE

$\frac{1}{2}$ cup salad oil
$\frac{1}{4}$ cup vinegar
1 tsp salt

1 tsp freshly ground pepper
2 tsp steak sauce *or* Worcester sauce
$\frac{1}{4}$ cup chopped onion

Mix all ingredients in a deep bowl. Add meat and stir to coat. Refrigerate overnight or let stand at room temperature 2-3 hours. This is good with barbecued kebabs, steak and chops.

♦ RED WINE MARINADE *(for game)*

2 small onions, sliced
2 sticks celery, chopped into chunks
sprig of fresh marjoram *or* pinch of
    dried marjoram
sprig of fresh thyme *or* pinch of
    dried thyme

2 medium carrots, sliced thinly
1 clove garlic, crushed
2 bay leaves
2 dsp black peppercorns, crushed
red wine
$1\frac{1}{2}$ cups oil

Mix all ingredients except wine and oil in a dish. Lay meat on top of mixture and pour in enough wine just to cover. Pour the oil over and leave for 24 hours or longer. This marinade can be used for a casserole or for a leg roast after marinating.

♦ PARSLEY BUTTER *(for use with grilled steaks or chops)*

50g butter
$\frac{1}{4}$ tsp salt

1 tbsp finely chopped parsley
1 tbsp lemon juice

Cream all ingredients togther thoroughly. Chill well.

Pickles and Chutneys

PICKLES AND CHUTNEYS

Before pickling, some vegetables require brining to remove some of the water they contain. Otherwise this liquid will dilute the pickling vinegar, making it cloudy and resulting in a pickle that will not keep well. Fruit is not brined.

Dry brining is suitable for very watery vegetables such as cucumber, marrow, and tomatoes. Place the prepared vegetables in a deep bowl in layers, sprinkling salt between the layers. Cover and leave overnight. Only a small amount of salt is needed – $\frac{1}{2}$ tablespoonful to 500g of vegetables.

Wet brining is suitable for vegetables such as cauliflower, onions and shallots. Allow 50g salt to 575ml water (sufficient for about 500g vegetables). Place the prepared vegetables in a deep bowl, cover with the brine and leave overnight. Root vegetables such as artichokes and beetroot must be cooked in half-strength brine until they are tender. After brining, rinse the vegetables thoroughly and drain them. If it is not possible to pickle them immediately, they may be placed in a fresh brine, made like the first one, and left until required.

◆ SPICED VINEGAR FOR PICKLING

1.75 *litres* vinegar
1 tbsp peppercorns
4 red chillies
6 slices root ginger

2 tsp mustard seed
8 cloves
1 tsp blade mace
1 clove garlic, crushed

Pour vinegar into a saucepan. Tie the spices and crushed garlic in a muslin bag and add to the pan, bring slowly to the boil and boil for five minutes, then leave for three hours or longer. Before using, remove the spice bag. Bottle the vinegar if not required at once. For such things as cocktail onions, white vinegar is usually used.

◆ PRE DINNER PICKLES

$2\frac{1}{4}$ cups sugar
$2\frac{1}{4}$ cups white vinegar
1 tsp salt
$1\frac{1}{4}$ cups water
1 cup cauliflower florets
2 medium carrots

1 cucumber
1 red capsicum
1 green capsicum
4 sticks celery (no tops)
8 shallots *or* small onions
small piece fresh ginger

In a saucepan, bring the sugar, vinegar, salt and water to the boil. Chop vegetables into bite-size pieces, add ginger unchopped. Boil a large saucepan of water and blanch vegetables. Drain by spreading on paper towel on wire rack. Pack in jars, cover with brine and seal. Store in fridge and leave at least a week.

◆ GREEN TOMATO MINCE

3kg green tomatoes
salt
1.5kg sugar

1kg raisins *or* sultanas
1/2kg currants
1 tsp cinnamon

Cut tomatoes, sprinkle over with salt and leave to draw off liquid. Drain off liquid. Place tomatoes in pan with all other ingredients. Boil 30 minutes. Seal while hot. Makes 7-8 jars. Use as pie filling.

◆ PICKLED GHERKINS

gherkins
1 cup sugar

1/2 tsp salt
1 *litre* spiced vinegar

Wash and wipe gherkins and pack into jars. Dissolve sugar and salt in vinegar and simmer for 3 minutes. Cool and pour warm mixture over gherkins to cover. Can be sealed or stored in jars with non-metallic screw lids.

◆ CUCUMBER RELISH

500g apples
500*ml* vinegar
500g sugar
1 tbsp salt
1 tsp pepper

1 dsp curry powder
750g onions, minced
750g cucumber, minced
tumeric

Mince apples and cook them in vinegar. When soft add sugar, salt, pepper, curry powder and minced onions. Bring to boil, add minced cucumber and boil 5 minutes. To colour add a little tumeric. Bottle and seal.

◆ RHUBARB CHUTNEY

1kg rhubarb
500g sultanas
1kg brown sugar
2 lemons
30g garlic

1 tbsp plain salt
500*ml* vinegar
1/4 tsp cayenne
30g dried ginger

Boil all ingredients for 1-1 1/2 hours, stirring frequently until mixture is thick. Bottle and seal when cold.

◆ CUCUMBER PICKLE

1 cup salt	³/₄ cup flour
1.75kg cucumbers, sliced	1 cup sugar
1.75kg onions, sliced	6 tbsp mustard
cold water to cover	1 tbsp tumeric
2.75 *litres* vinegar	extra vinegar

Sprinkle salt on sliced cucumbers and onions. Cover with cold water and stand for 24 hours. Boil vinegar, add drained cucumber and onions, boil until tender. Mix flour, sugar, mustard and tumeric to a smooth paste with vinegar, add and boil for a few minutes. Bottle and seal while hot. Makes 7 jars of pickle.

◆ BREAD AND BUTTER PICKLE

10-12 cups thinly sliced unpeeled gherkins *or* cucumbers	4 cups sugar
6 onions, sliced	1 tbsp mustard seed
½ cup non-iodised salt	2 tsp celery seed
4 cups white vinegar	1-2 tsp tumeric
	1 red capsicum, cut into thin strips

Cover gherkins or cucumbers, onions and salt with cold water and leave overnight. Drain, rinse with cold water and drain again. In a large saucepan boil vinegar with remaining ingredients, stirring until sugar dissolves. Reduce heat and simmer for 5 minutes. Pack vegetables into hot sterilised jars. Add red capsicum to each jar, if wished. Fill with vinegar mixture to 1cm from top. Cover with non-metallic lid when cold.

◆ MUSTARD PICKLE

1kg onions	1 *litre* white vinegar
6 tbsp plain salt	2½ cups white sugar
1kg cauliflower	4 tbsp flour
1kg cucumber	4 tbsp mustard
1kg beans	1 dsp tumeric
1kg green tomatoes	vinegar

Cut up onions, put into basin and sprinkle with 2 tablespoons of the salt, cover with water and leave overnight. In another basin cut up the vegetables and sprinkle with 4 tablespoons salt, cover with water and leave overnight. Drain, rinse under cold tap and drain again. Place all vegetables in a pan, add white vinegar and sugar, and boil rapidly for 10 minutes. Thicken with flour, mustard and tumeric mixed with a little vinegar. Bring to boil and bottle hot. Leave until cold before putting lids on. For crisp vegetables, don't boil too long after thickening.

PICKLES CHUTNEYS

145

♦ PICKLE PIQUANT

1.75g tomatoes
4 cups chopped celery
500g onions, chopped
4 cups chopped cucumber
¾ cup salt
8 cups hot water

4 cups vinegar
6 cups sugar
4 tbsp mustard
2 tbsp tumeric
1½ cups flour

Cut up tomatoes and put in bowl. Put celery, onions and cucumber in a separate bowl. Mix salt and water and and pour over. Leave overnight. Drain off brine and also liquid from tomatoes. Bring 2 cups of the vinegar and all the sugar to the boil in preserving pan. Mix all dry ingredients with remaining 2 cups of vinegar, add to pan, stirring to prevent lumps. Add vegetables and heat until just boiling. Bottle.

♦ TAMARILLO CHUTNEY

24 tamarillos
boiling water
450g apples, chopped
900g onions, chopped
900g brown sugar

575*ml* vinegar
2 tbsp salt
3 tbsp allspice
1 tsp cayenne

Place tamarillos in boiling water and remove skins. Chop roughly and add to all other ingredients in a saucepan. Boil for at least an hour stirring frequently until thick and jam-like. Bottle.

♦ PICKLED ONIONS

Use small pickling onions. Remove skins carefully without cutting onions, wash and soak in brine for 24 hours. Drain, wash and dry and place in jars. Fill up jars with cold spiced vinegar and cover. Store in a cool dry place.

♦ BEETROOT CHUTNEY

1kg cooked beetroot, minced
500g onion, minced
2 cups sugar
1 tsp ground allspice
5 peppercorns

1 tbsp salt
vinegar
3 tbsp cornflour
water

Put all ingredients in a saucepan, except cornflour and water, with sufficient vinegar to cover. Boil for 25 minutes. Thicken with the cornflour mixed to a smooth paste with a little water and boil for 5 minutes more. Put into jars and seal when cold.

◆ PLUM CHUTNEY

5kg plums
1kg onions, sliced
3kg sugar
1dsp salt
50g whole pickling spices
vinegar

Place plums, onion, sugar and salt in pan with spices tied in muslin. Barely cover with vinegar. Boil about 2 hours or until plums and onions are soft and mixture thick. Put into clean jars and seal when cold.

◆ TOMATO RELISH

12 medium ripe tomatoes
6 medium onions
1 cup white sugar
560*ml* vinegar
1 tbsp salt
½ tbsp mustard
½ tbsp curry powder
3 tbsp flour
water

In a saucepan, boil all ingredients, except flour and water, for 1 hour. Mix flour to a paste with a little water. Add to saucepan and bring to boil to thicken. Bottle and seal when cold.

◆ APPLE AND TOMATO CHUTNEY

2kg tomatoes
2kg sour apples, peeled, cored
  and chopped
1kg onions, chopped
2 cloves garlic, peeled and chopped
500g brown sugar
2 tbsp salt
1 tsp cayenne

Blanch, peel and chop tomatoes. In a saucepan cover all ingredients with vinegar and boil slowly for about 4 hours or until thick and jam-like. Bottle and seal when cold.

◆ RHUBARB AND ONION CHUTNEY

2.5kg rhubarb, chopped
2.5kg onions, chopped
1kg apples, unpeeled, chopped
1.5kg sugar
1 tsp curry powder
¼ tsp pepper
1 dsp ground cloves
1 tsp mustard
1 dsp ground ginger
2 dsp plain salt
1.125 *litres* vinegar

Put rhubarb, onions and apples with other ingredients in a saucepan and boil for 3 hours, stirring frequently. Bottle and seal when cold.

Jams, Jellies, Conserves, Preserving

JAMS, JELLIES, CONSERVES, PRESERVING

HINTS ON JAM MAKING
There are two general methods of making jam:

The fruit and sugar are cooked together: This method gives a jam with pieces of fruit in it. Sometimes the fruit and sugar are left together overnight for juices to form before making into jam.

The fruit is cooked until it soft and then the warmed sugar is added: This jam has a more even texture and the pulp is evenly distributed throughout the jam.

Setting test
Testing for setting should be done first when the jam no longer runs off the spoon but drops in clots. Put about a teaspoon of jam on a clean cold saucer and allow it to cool (about three minutes). Tilt the saucer and if the surface of the jam wrinkles as a result, the jam will set. Alternatively, draw a finger through the jam and if the channel thus made does not run together jam is ready to set.

Faults in jam
♦ Thin, running jam: Too much water has been added; or there was not enough pectin or acid in the fruit; or the jam was not boiled long enough.
♦ Very thick, brownish jam with a caramel flavour: Overcooked.
♦ Sugar crystals on top of jam: Not properly cooked or excess sugar.
♦ Mould on top of jam: Not enough sugar; not enough boiling, or jars not properly covered.

Tips
♦ It is much easier and quicker to make up small quantities of jam than one large quantity – it's wiser not to make up more than 2 kg of fruit at a time.
♦ Grease the bottom of the pan to prevent burning.
♦ Instead of skimming jam, drop in a piece of butter the size of a walnut before bottling.
♦ Pack jam into hot, dry jars. Cover when cold.

♦ APRICOT JAM

425*ml* water
juice of 1 lemon

1.75kg apricots, stoned and chopped
1.75kg sugar

Put the water, lemon juice and apricots, with some of the apricot kernels, in a pan and bring to the boil. Cook until tender and then add the sugar. Bring back to the boil and boil hard until it gives a setting test. Pot the jam, cover and label.

♦ DRIED APRICOT JAM

450g dried apricots
1.75 *litres* water

1.25kg sugar
1x 225g can crushed pineapple (optional)

Wash the apricots and soak them in the water for at least 24 hours. Put on to boil and boil until soft. Add pineapple if used. Add sugar and boil until setting test is given.

♦ APRICOT PULP JAM

2 cups water
2.25kg apricot pulp

2.25kg sugar
1 x 400g can crushed pineapple

Put water and pulp in pan and bring to the boil. Add sugar and pineapple and boil until setting test is given.

♦ SAGE JELLY

2 cups apple juice
1½ cups sugar
juice of 2 lemons

1 small handful sage
extra sage leaves

To apple juice add sugar, the lemon juice and sage. Stir and lightly crush the sage to extract flavour as you bring to the boil, then allow to boil freely until it will set. Pour into jars adding a fresh sage leaf to each jar. Best with pork and poultry.

♦ BLACKBERRY AND APPLE JELLY

1.75kg blackberries
900g cooking apples

1.25 *litres* water
sugar

Wash the blackberries and put in the pan with the apples, cut up but not peeled or cored, and water. Simmer until tender. Mash well and strain the fruit through a jelly bag. Measure the juice and add cup for cup of sugar. Stir well and boil rapidly until it gives a setting test.

♦ PLUM CONSERVE

2 thin-skinned oranges, pips removed
1.5kg fresh plums, stoned and
   quartered

1.5kg raw sugar
500g raisins
225g walnuts, chopped

Mince oranges in food processor. In large, heavy saucepan or pan, combine oranges, plums, sugar and raisins. Cook, stirring occasionally until mixture is very thick, about 1 hour. Stir in nuts and cook a further 20 minutes. Pour into hot sterilised jars. Cover and cool.

♦ BLACKCURRANT JAM

900g blackcurrants   575*ml* water
1.35kg sugar

Boil fruit and water for five minutes. Add sugar and boil hard for 10 minutes. If these directions are followed, no testing is necessary. The jam will gel excellently.

♦ CAPE GOOSEBERRY JAM

1.75kg cape gooseberries   sugar
water

Place the fruit in pan and barely cover with water. Boil until the skins are tender. Add cup for cup of sugar and pulp and boil until it gives a setting test.

♦ PEAR AND GINGER JAM

1.35kg pears, peeled and cored   juice and grated rind of 2 lemons
225g preserved ginger   1.35kg sugar

Cut up pears into small pieces. Chop the ginger and add with the juice and grated rind of the lemons. Put all ingredients in a pan and let stand overnight. Bring to boil, stirring slowly. Boil slowly until the pears are clear and the mixture thick, about 2 hours.

♦ QUINCE CONSERVE

2.75kg quinces, peeled and quartered   2.75kg sugar
675g sugar   water

Place quinces in a pan, barely cover with water and cook until soft. Lift fruit out into basin and cover with the 675g sugar. Set aside for 12 hours. Boil peelings and cores with liquid from quinces for 1 hour. Strain and add the 2.75kg sugar. Bring to boil again and add quinces. Boil until syrup jellies, about ½ hour.

♦ RASPBERRY JAM

butter   1.75kg sugar
1.75kg raspberries

Butter preserving pan well. Put in fruit and gradually bring to boil, stirring to avoid sticking. Add warmed sugar, and boil quickly for 3 minutes. (Warm sugar in roasting pan in a low oven.)

♦ GRAPE JELLY

grapes   sugar

Wash grapes and place them, without any water at all, in a pan and mash them down with a potato masher. Bring to the boil, stirring frequently and boil until pulped. Strain through a sieve, pressing down hard with the back of a spoon. Measure the liquid and add cup for cup of sugar. Boil as hard as possible to 220°C or until a little on a saucer will set.

♦ RASPBERRY PLUM JAM

1.35kg plums   1.25kg sugar
1 chip raspberries

Boil fruit until soft, add sugar and boil briskly until setting test is given.

♦ KIWIFRUIT JAM

1.25kg kiwifruit, peeled and chopped   50g preserved ginger, chopped small
3 cups water   1.25kg sugar
juice and rind of 1 lemon

Boil kiwifruit and water in a pan until soft. Add rind and juice of lemon and the ginger. Boil again and then add sugar and boil quickly until mixture gives setting test.

♦ FRUIT SALAD JAM

1.35kg apricots   2 oranges
1 x 400g can pineapple pieces   2.25kg sugar
2 lemons

Put apricots and pineapple cut into small pieces in pan. Add grated rind and juice of lemons and oranges. Boil five minutes without sugar. Add sugar and boil until it sets when tested.

♦ GOOSEBERRY JAM

1.35kg gooseberries   2.25kg sugar
600*ml* water

Top and tail gooseberries and place them in a preserving pan with the water. Cook until fruit is tender. Add sugar and boil hard until it sets when tested.

♦ FEIJOA JAM

900g feijoas
140*ml* water

1 lemon
900g sugar

Peel and slice feijoas. Add water and juice of lemon and boil until tender. Add sugar and boil until it sets when tested.

♦ GRAPE SYRUP

grapes
water

sugar

Put grapes in pan and half cover with water. Cook until pulped. Strain. Add cup of sugar for each cup of juice and boil hard until thick and syrupy. Bottle. An excellent topping for ice cream, pancakes or waffles, or as a flavouring in drinks.

♦ MARMALADE

450g citrus fruit (grapefruit,
orange, lemon)

1.75 *litres* water
1.35kg sugar

Cut up fruit and soak in water overnight. (All grapefruit may be used or grapefruit with lemon and/or orange). Boil until tender. Add sugar and boil hard until it sets when tested.

♦ RHUBARB AND ORANGE JAM

2 oranges
1.35kg rhubarb, chopped
water

1 tsp ground ginger
1.35kg sugar

Grate rind of oranges, peel off white pith and discard. Cut up flesh and put into a basin with rhubarb. Cover with water and let stand overnight. Bring to the boil and boil for about 15 minutes or until soft. Add sugar and continue boiling until setting test is given. Add ginger and stir well. Bottle while hot.

♦ CRABAPPLE JELLY

1.75kg crabapples
1.25 *litres* water

a few cloves (optional)
sugar

Wash crabapples and cut in quarters, without peeling or coring. Put in pan with water and simmer until mushy. Add more water if necessary. Add cloves while cooking if liked. Strain through a jelly cloth. Do not squeeze bag. Measure juice and put in pan. Bring to boil, then add 350-450g sugar to each 575*ml* liquid. Stir while sugar is dissolving, allow to boil briskly about 10 minutes without stirring, then test for jellying. As soon as it gels, pot and cover.

♦ PLUM AND MINT JELLY *(serve with roast lamb or game)*

1.35kg dark red plums	225g demerara sugar to every
150*ml* wine vinegar	275*ml* juice
425*ml* water	6 tbsp chopped mint

Wipe plums, slit all round. Put in preserving pan with vinegar and water. Bring to boil, simmer about 45 minutes until very soft, stirring occasionally. Mash as they soften. Remove stones which float to top. Strain through muslin. Let drip at least 2 hours. Measure juice. Weigh appropriate amount of warmed sugar. Pour juice into clean pan and boil. Add sugar, stir until dissolved. Boil again to setting point. Take pan from heat. Stir in the mint. Cool mixture to lukewarm. Stir again to distribute mint. Pour into warm pots. Cover with waxed paper circles. When quite cold, cover with cellophane or lids.

♦ PRESERVING

The fresher the fruit, the better it preserves. This applies especially to soft fruit such as raspberries. The ideal condition for fruits being preserved is just before they reach full ripeness. If over-ripe they are likely to lose all shape when heated, and squash down in the bottle. If under-ripe, they will not have gained full flavour.

If it must be done, it doesn't matter about picking fruit on a rainy day – but the fruit must be bottled at once.

Gooseberries are bottled when green (i.e. under-ripe); other fruits when firm-ripe.

Always try to complete preserving on the same day that the fruit is picked, especially with soft fruits and all berries.

Grading
Each individual fruit must be sound, healthy, unbruised, unblemished, and with skin that is whole and uncut. Fruit should be graded into size and degree of ripeness so that all in one bottle are of a similar size, shape and colour. Grading is of extreme importance if the products are intended for exhibition.

Washing
Fruit must be clean, preferably not dusty or gritty, and certainly not gathered in dirty baskets. Wash fruit in a colander, allowing water to pour on the fruit and drain away. Large fruit, such as plums, may be wiped with a cloth. Small berry fruits, such as raspberries, will not stand treatment in a colander. These are best washed after packing them in the jar by filling the jar with water and then inverting it, allowing the water to run out between the fingers of the hand which is held over the mouth of the jar to prevent the contents escaping.

Removing skins
Tomatoes, peaches and plums of the variety of which the skins split on heating, usually have the skins removed. Pip fruits are peeled with a knife. The simplest plan is to gather up the fruit in a colander or butter-muslin bag and hold in boiling water for 20-60 seconds according to variety. Then take out and cool as quickly as possible in a large basin of cold water. The skins can then be peeled off with a knife or slipped off with the fingers.

Preserving methods

Water bath method: This method is recommended because it ensures the brightest colour, the finest flavour, the firmest texture, retention of the original shape and the most attractive appearance in the finished product. This is the best method for exhibition. The essential steps are: (1) Provide clean, sound bottles. (2) Prepare and grade clean, unblemished fruit. (3) Pack firmly into bottles. (4) Fill with covering liquid to the brim. (5) Adjust seals and screw bands. (6) Place in a steriliser or in a water bath so that jars are covered by water. (7) Heat to the correct temperature and for proper length of time. (8) Take out of water, adjust screw bands and allow to cool. (9) Test for effective sealing. (10) Label and store away.

Open pan method: With this method: (1) Fruit is stewed in syrup and while boiling packed into hot sterilised jars to completely fill and just overflow. (2) Release any air pockets with a skewer or knife. (3) Clear rim of any fruit particles and seal. (4) Check seal when cold. This method is only suitable for fruit.

Boiling water method: This method is satisfactory for gooseberries, some plums and the acid fruits. It is quick and therefore most useful if time is precious just when the fruit is right for preserving.

Gooseberries must be green and sour though well developed; plums must be of the cooking varieties and firm-ripe. (1) Pack the clean selected prepared fruit in hot preserving jars. (2) Fill with boiling water, count 15 seconds and pour off. (3) Fill again with boiling water, count 10 seconds and pour off. (4) Fill a third time with boiling water and immediately affix caps airtight. (5) Allow jars to cool gradually and store away.

Hot and Cold Drinks

HOT AND COLD DRINKS

To be appetising a cold drink must be *really* cold, so keep a good supply of ice cubes, milk and a large bottle of water in the refrigerator for use in cool drinks. For an extra flourish, serve ice cubes brightly coloured with colourings or ice cubes in which have been frozen garnishes such as cherries, mint sprigs and grapes. Lemon or orange squash or juice can be frozen as ice cubes. An additional attraction is provided by frosting the rims of glasses by dipping them first to a depth of 6mm in lightly beaten egg-white or lemon juice, then in coloured sugar.

◆ ORANGE MILK SHAKE *(fat-free)*

1 serving:
½ cup orange juice
2-4 tbsp non-fat dried milk

1-2 ice-blocks (optional)

Shake the juice, milk powder and ice together in a cocktail shaker or screw-topped jar and drink immediately. A spoonful of vanilla instant pudding mix may be added if desired.

◆ COUNTRY CLUB PUNCH

3 cups sugar
4 *litres* water
1 cup strong tea
12 lemons
12 oranges

860*ml* apple juice
1 x 225g can crushed pineapple
2.5 *litres* ginger ale
ice cubes

Boil the sugar and water together for 8 minutes. Add the tea and then chill. Add juice of lemons and oranges, apple juice and pineapple. Place in the refrigerator to mellow for about two hours. Before serving add ginger ale and ice cubes. If served in a punch bowl add slices of orange and lemon and 1 small bottle of cherries. Serves about 50.

◆ FRUIT PUNCH

2 cups strong cold strained tea
1 cup grape juice

6 cups mixed fruit juice
1 large bottle lemonade *or* ginger ale

Mix tea and juices and chill. Add lemonade to other ingredients just before serving.

DRINKS

157

♦ MILK SHAKES

Have 1 cup milk thoroughly chilled. Shake or beat with fruit or other flavouring and ice cream until well blended.

Banana: Use half a mashed banana.

Strawberry: Use ¼ cup crushed sweetened strawberries.

Chocolate: Use 1½ -2 tbsp chocolate syrup made from boiling water with cocoa and honey.

Honey and peanut butter: One tsp of honey and 1 tsp peanut butter whipped up in a blender with milk.

♦ BLACKCURRANT DRINK

2kg blackcurrants
2.75kg sugar

3.5 *litres* water
1 dsp tartaric acid

Boil fruit with water for 12 minutes. Remove from heat, mash and strain. Return liquid with sugar added to heat and boil another 12 minutes. Remove from heat and add tartaric acid. Bottle in dry sterilised containers and seal.

♦ MOCK CHAMPAGNE

1 cup sugar
1 cup water
1 cup grapefruit juice

½ cup orange juice
¼ cup lemon juice
1 *litre* ginger ale

Combine sugar and water in saucepan and boil for five minutes. Cool. Stir in well chilled fruit juices. Add ginger ale.

♦ ICED TEA

ice cubes
strong tea
lemon *or* orange slices

icing sugar
mint leaves

Put 2-3 ice cubes in each glass. Pour strong, fresh, cold tea on cubes. Add slices of lemon or orange and sweeten with icing sugar. For minted tea, put several bruised leaves of mint in each glass. Pour the hot tea over and chill. Add ice cubes.

♦ ICED COFFEE

coffee

milk or cream or ice cream

Make fresh coffee (or use left-over coffee). When cold, store in a corked bottle in the refrigerator. When required, serve with chilled milk, whipped cream or with a spoonful of vanilla ice cream whipped into it.

♦ GINGER BEER (1)

4 cups sugar
1 tsp tartaric acid
1 dsp ground ginger

juice of 3 lemons
6 *litres* cold water
sultanas

Place sugar, tartaric acid, ground ginger, lemon juice and water in a large bowl and stir until the sugar is dissolved. Strain through a muslin cloth. Bottle. Drop three sultanas into each bottle and seal securely. When sultanas rise to the top, the ginger beer is ready to drink, approximately 3-4 days.

♦ GINGER BEER (2)

1 dsp sugar
2 cups water

1 dsp ginger
1 tbsp lemon juice

Feeding:

sugar
ground ginger
sugar

water
lemons
raisins

Combine together all the ingredients. On days 1, 3, 5 and 7 add 1 dessertspoon sugar. On days 2, 4 and 6 add 1 dessertspoon ground ginger. On day 8 dissolve 2 cups of sugar in 4 cups hot water, add the juice of 2 lemons and 12 cups of cold water, and add liquid from beer plant. Stir to combine the liquid and the syrup then bottle with 2 raisins in each bottle and seal tight. Split the sediment remaining and start another plant with one half of the sediment. Discard the rest or give it away.

♦ LEMON SQUASH

2¹/₂ cups sugar
1 *litre* boiling water
2 tbsp tartaric acid

juice of 3 lemons
grated lemon rind

Dissolve the sugar in the water. Add the juice and grated rind of the lemons. Add the tartaric acid. Bottle and store in the refrigerator. Dilute with water or soda water to taste.

♦ ORANGE SQUASH

Use Lemon Squash recipe with 3 oranges and 1 lemon.

DRINKS

Cooking
for a Crowd

Cooking for a large number of people requires planning:
♦ Ascertain the number of people attending the function being catered for

♦ Decide on the kinds of food to be served

♦ Work out when you will require food to be ready for picking up or delivering to the function

♦ Consider the number of helpers you will require.

♦ USEFUL HINTS

♦ One 200g jar instant coffee serves 150 people. 500g tea serves approximately 200 people.

♦ 1 litre milk serves tea or coffee for approximately 40 people.

♦ 1 sliced 900g sandwich loaf averages 20-24 slices suitable for use . . .and this will require 170-200g butter for spreading.

♦ Bread for asparagus rolls can be made easier to roll by steaming for 2-3 minutes in a covered colander. Cool bread before buttering.

♦ Garlic butter can be quickly made up using 2 teaspoons garlic stock powder per 500g butter.

♦ Make garlic bread by diagonally slicing a French loaf or bread stick, cutting almost to the base but not right through. Spread garlic butter both sides, wrap in aluminium foil and place in 180°C oven for 15-20 minutes or until hot. Allow one bread stick to 4-5 people, depending on length and number of cuts.

♦ Each 750g sandwich loaf will make approximately 30 club sandwiches (i.e. 4 bread slices, 3 fillings, each set of sandwiches cut into 6 club sandwiches).

♦ 6-8 eggs mixed with salad dressing will fill a loaf of sandwiches.

♦ For salads allow 100g per person (i.e. 1kg of salad will feed 10 people).

♦ For a morning or afternoon tea, allow 3 sandwiches and 2 pieces of cake per person.

♦ Cakes: One sponge sandwich will supply 12 slices; a 450g fruitcake, 20 slices.

♦ One 1.125 litre container of ice cream contains 18 helpings.

Suggested food quantities for	20 people	50 people
Coffee	40g	100g
Tea	40g	100g
Canned food	2.5kg	6kg
Rice (uncooked)	600g	1.5kg
Fish fillets	2.5kg	7kg
Cold sliced meat	1.25kg	3.5kg
Casserole steak	2.5kg	7kg
Turkey	7kg	2 x 9kg
Chicken	3-4	6-8
Milk for tea/coffee	600*ml*	2 x 600*ml*
Sugar for tea/coffee	200g	500g
Butter	200g	500g
Cream to whip	600ml	1.5 *litres*
Ice cream	3 litres	7 *litres*

♦ The number of servings suggested with the recipes following are approximate only; actual servings will depend on the 'audience', their appetites and accompaniments are on the menu. A team of footballers should eat more than a family gathering that has children among its members . . . though not necessarily!

♦ CATERING FOR BUFFET MEAL (*serves 50*)

9 sandwich loaves
13 loaves garlic bread
9 dinner plate-sized pizzas
12 tins smoked fish (with white sauce and vegetables added)
4 x No.10 chickens cooked in casserole with vegetables

17 dozen savouries
250 cheerios
3kg mince, curried
3.5 *litres* milk
salt and pepper
2 packets toothpicks
tomato sauce

Dress tables with small dishes of potato chips and nuts.

♦ SUPPER FOR ONE HUNDRED

club sandwiches	10 dozen
asparagus rolls	8 dozen
sausage rolls	9 dozen
savouries	9 dozen
savoury eggs	8 dozen halves
5 large chickens	
1 ham	
cherrios	10 dozen
cream sponges	10 halves
chocolate eclairs	8 dozen
lamingtons	8 dozen
meringues	6 dozen

♦ CRAYFISH DIP (*serves 12*)

200g cream cheese
1 cup cooked and flaked crayfish
1/2 cup sour cream *or* salad dressing
1/2 tsp salt
onion juice

lemon juice
2 tbsp blue vein cheese
top milk
chives

Soften cream cheese, add remaining ingredients, thin to dip consistency with top milk if required. Serve in bowls on platter with cheese biscuits, rye wafers, potato chips, suitable snack biscuits.

♦ COLESLAW (*serves 12*)

1 large firm white cabbage,
    shredded finely
4 large carrots
1 large onion

1 cup diced celery
1/2 cup oil, oil and vinegar,
    or salad dressing

Shred all vegetables in food processor for ease of preparation. Add oil and vinegar and let stand to develop flavour for 30-60 minutes. Try adding radish and capsicum for variety.

♦ POTATO SALAD FOR A CROWD (*serves 12*)

2kg cooked potato, diced
3 hard-boiled eggs
1 tbsp chopped parsley
1 tbsp chopped chives

1 tsp chopped thyme
1 cup salad dressing
garlic salt *or* powder
salt and pepper

Combined ingredients while potatoes are still hot. Chill. Serve with other salads for variety. Cooked green beans, peas, peppers may be added for colour.

♦ RICE SALAD (*serves 12*)

6 cups cooked rice
1 x 425g can bean salad, drained
3 cooked rashers bacon, diced
1 capsicum, diced

1 cup celery, chopped
1 cup cheese, diced
1 onion, finely chopped

Dressing:

1 tbsp oil
2 tbsp vinegar
1 tsp brown sugar

salt and pepper
pinch of chilli powder
garlic powder

Combine ingredients and blend well. Add dressing. Refrigerate for at least 2 hours to develop flavour. Toss just before serving. Garnish with tomato slices and red onion rings.

♦ JELLIED BEETROOT SALAD (*serves 12*)

4 tbsp gelatine
2$^1/_2$ cups water
2 tbsp sugar
$^1/_2$ cup vinegar

1 tsp salt
pepper
1-1.5kg cooked beetroot, diced

Soften gelatine in a little of the water, add sugar, heat until dissolved, add vinegar, seasoning and water. Pour cold gelatine mixture over beetroot in a large bowl. Allow to set. Cut into squares and serve on plates or as garnish for cold meat salad.

♦ PUNCH (*serves 50*)

1 *litre* cold tea
2$^1/_2$ cups sugar
2 *litres* orange juice
2 *litres* pineapple juice
2 *litres* apple and orange juice

juice of 2 lemons
750*ml* grapefruit juice
2 x 1.25 *litre* bottles ginger ale
sprigs of mint
ice cubes

Simmer tea and sugar to dissolve sugar, add juices and bring to boil. Chill thoroughly. Add chilled ginger ale and serve with sprig of mint and ice cubes.

♦ APPLE, CELERY AND WALNUT SALAD (*serves 16*)

2.5kg apples
4 cups chopped celery

170g walnuts, chopped
2 cups salad dressing

Wash, core and chop apples. Combine with other ingredients and toss lightly. Chill to serve.

◆ ELLA'S SQUARE (*serves about 40*)

450g butter
3 cups sugar
4 cups flour
4 tbsp cocoa

3 tsp baking powder
4 cups coconut
4 cups sultanas or raisins
chocolate icing

Cream together butter and sugar. Sift and add flour, cocoa, and baking powder. Add coconut and sultanas or raisins. Cook in large meat dish or 2 sponge roll tins at 180°C for 45 minutes for large tin or 30 minutes for smaller tins. Cut into pieces. Ice with chocolate icing.

◆ STRAWBERRY ICE CREAM SLICE (*serves 24*)

1 slab of caterer's sponge *or*
    2 lamington sponges
1 x 1 *litre* packet vanilla ice-cream slices

strawberries
sugar (optional)

Cut each sponge into two layers horizontally. Put one layer into bottom of sponge roll tin lined with foil. Layer sponge with half the strawberries, and sugar if desired. Take ice cream slices and layer on to strawberries. Cover with another layer of strawberries. Top with remaining sponge. Cover with foil and freeze.

◆ CHEESE SPREAD (*for sandwiches*)

125g cheese, grated
1 egg, beaten
$1/2$ tsp salt
$1/2$ tsp pepper
$1/2$ tsp mustard

1 tbsp vinegar
1 tbsp cream or butter
pinch curry powder (optional)
garlic powder (optional)

In a saucepan bring all ingredients to boiling point gently, stirring constantly. Add a little curry powder if liked. Bottle and refrigerate.

◆ CREAMED SMOKED FISH (*serves 30*)

125g butter
1 large onion, chopped
$1/2$ tsp curry powder
5 tbsp flour
salt and pepper

575-860*ml* milk
4 x 225g cans smoked fish
9-12 hard-boiled eggs
2 cups mixed vegetables

Melt butter, add onion. Cook gently with curry until clear. Add flour, pepper and salt, then add milk until sauce is good consistency. Add smoked fish, eggs and vegetables.

♦ CHICKEN CASSEROLE FOR A CROWD (*serves 35*)

2 large chickens
2 onions, chopped
1kg mixed vegetables
1 packet mushroom soup powder

1 packet cream of chicken soup powder
6 tbsp cornflour

Cook chickens, bone, and flake meat. Reserve 2.25 *litres* chicken stock and set and skim. Put stock into large pot and add onions and mixed vegetables. Cook until nearly done, strain liquid, reserving stock and thicken with soups and cornflour. When thick, add vegetables and chicken.

♦ MINCE CURRY (*serves 25*)

1 tbsp oil
1 clove garlic
1 onion, chopped
2 tsp strong curry powder
$^1/_4$ tsp ginger
$^1/_4$ tsp mixed spice
$^1/_4$ tsp cinnamon
$^1/_4$ tsp mixed herbs
1.5 kg mince

1 x 425g can crushed pineapple
1 dsp brown sugar
$^3/_4$ cup sultanas
$^1/_4$ cup tomato sauce
1 tbsp Worcester sauce
2 tbsp soy sauce
1 tbsp vinegar
2 packets Maggi brown onion sauce
diced mixed vegetables, (optional)

Fry oil, garlic, onion, curry powder and spices together. Add mince and brown. Add crushed pineapple, brown sugar and sultanas. When well browned add tomato sauce, Worcester sauce, soy sauce and vinegar. Add water until right consistency and thicken with brown onion sauce. Add vegetables if liked. Best made the day before and left in fridge.

♦ CURRY FOR A CROWD (*serves 20-25*)

2.5kg stewing steak, cubed
500g apples, chopped
500g sultanas
2 tbsp salt
3 tsp curry powder or to taste
500g onions, chopped
1 cup coconut
100g butter

1 x 1kg packet frozen mixed vegetables
$^1/_2$ cup chopped celery
3 tbsp chutney *or* plum jam
1 tsp ginger
$1^1/_2$ tsp mustard mixed with water
1 tbsp cornflour
2 tbsp water

Brown first 7 ingredients in the butter. Cover with water and simmer until cooked. Add frozen mixed vegetables and celery, chutney or plum jam. Add ginger, mustard and cornflour mixed with a little water. Thicken liquid with mixed paste. For a sweeter curry add pineapple or chopped peaches.

♦ BEEF GOULASH (*serves about 30*)

6.75kg gravy beef
340g butter
salt and pepper to taste
6 medium onions, diced
2 cups flour
3 tbsp paprika

3.4 *litres* stock *or* water
1 tsp marjoram
3-4 bay leaves
570*ml* sour cream
chopped parsley
1 x 425g can tomato juice

Cut meat into cubes, fry until brown in pan with butter and seasoning. Remove from pan. Brown onions, add flour and paprika. Cook, stirring until smooth. Add stock and stir until sauce thickens, adding seasoning to taste. Put meat back into gravy and cook until tender, about 2 hours. Add sour cream and parsley just before serving.

Handy Hints

FREEZER HINTS

♦ When **kiwifruit** are plentiful, peel surplus fruit, slice and place in plastic bags to freeze. These can then be thawed and used in fruit salads or when required for a marinade.

♦ Keep **root ginger** in freezer and grate off sufficient at time of use.

♦ **Stewed apples** stored in plastic containers are as fresh as the day they are cooked.

♦ Whip **cream** before freezing – it stays whipped. As much as is required can then be cut off and thawed in a few minutes. The cream can also be piped into rosettes and other shapes before freezing.

There are some foods which do not take kindly to storage in the freezer, and so when preparing a programme of preparation and freezing, it is wise to remember the following points.

♦ **Garlic** tends to develop an 'off flavour' in frozen casseroles and stews, so do not include garlic in these dishes. Instead add garlic when reheating the dishes.

♦ **The flavour of onions** used in prepared dishes alters when these are stored in the freezer for a long time. Storage for up to a month is satisfactory however.

♦ **Salt** in excessive amounts inhibits the freezing of foods.

♦ **Peas** and **potatoes** should not be added to savoury dishes before freezing. Add when reheating.

♦ Toppings with **crumbs** and **cheese** should be added after thawing.

♦ **Cooked fish** is not recommended for freezing unless it is incorporated in fish cakes, fish pie and the like.

♦ The white of **hard-boiled eggs** becomes tough and rubbery when frozen.

♦ **Salad vegetables** such as lettuce, tomatoes, cucumbers, whole onions, celery and radishes lose their crispness when frozen and cannot be served in salads. However, tomatoes and celery that have been frozen can be cooked satisfactorily, and frozen chopped onions are handy for casseroles.

♦ **Avocados** do not freeze well, but when thawed are fine mashed with lemon juice for use in dips.

♦ **Salted cheese** that has been frozen cannot be served in a platter but can be used in cooking.

♦ Do not freeze **stuffed poultry.** Due to slow freezing of the stuffing it may harbour harmful bacteria that can cause illness when later thawed and eaten.

♦ Sauces thickened with **flour** thin on thawing. Use cornflour or rice flour to avoid this.

♦ **Custards, cream fillings** and **milk puddings** tend to curdle or separate if frozen. Caramel creams do *not* freeze and frozen **gelatine dishes** will separate on thawing.

♦ **Sour cream** separates when frozen on its own, but freezes satisfactorily when combined with other ingredients.

♦ **Precooked vegetables** tend to acquire a 'warmed up' flavour with freezing, but become more acceptable when served with a sauce.

♦ **Bananas** when frozen whole turn brown, but mashed with lemon juice can be used as fillings for sandwiches or making cakes.

♦ Do not place **hot foods** in freezer; leave to cool before freezing.

♦ Instead of freezing **tomatoes** whole, pulp them, put through a sieve, cool, and pack meal-sized quantities in containers. It saves a lot of space in the freezer and they are ready for use when thawed.

♦ **In case of a power blackout** keep the freezer closed as much as possible. The contents of a well-stocked freezer will keep safely frozen for about 24 hours in the event of trouble, provided the freezer is kept tightly closed. Put ice cream packed in cardboard into plastic bags because they are first to thaw and if they run, make quite a mess.
If partial thawing has occurred before refrigeration is resumed you can re-freeze any packages in which some ice still remains. However, such packages should be used as soon as possible. Identify these for using first.
If complete thawing has occurred, various foods should be handled differently. For example, thawed fruits can be used for high quality jams, jellies, sauces or preserves. Completely thawed meats, poultry and fish should not be re-frozen and only used if still very cold and there are no signs of deterioration.

HOUSEHOLD HINTS

♦ If using **paint** that has a few lumps, place a stocking loosely over the top of the tin and push down with brush into paint. This prevents lumps getting into the bristles.

♦ To preserve the life of **silk garments**, wash without excessive rubbing, adding a dash of white vinegar to rinsing water. Vinegar removes all traces of soap residue and also adds a shine to garment.

♦ Lighting a match in the **toilet** after using helps to quickly eliminate strong odours.

♦ **Copper** comes up like new by using equal parts lemon juice and salt. Rinse and polish. Lemon juice can be substituted by vinegar.

♦ **Leftover wine** or **beer** is excellent in stews or casseroles.

- The strong flavour of **onion rings** is lessened and their crispness retained if they are soaked in iced, salted water an hour before adding to salads.

- Prick an **egg** with a needle at the round end to prevent cracking while boiling.

- **Scrambled eggs** will not become watery if 1 teaspoon of cornflour is added to the mixture.

- **Whipped cream** stays fresh for days if a pinch of baking soda is added while whipping.

- **Baked potatoes** will be crisper if they are brushed with oil or melted butter before baking.

- To quickly dry **herbs**, pluck the leaves from the stalks, wipe them clean (do *not* wash), place between paper towels and microwave on high for three minutes. Turn if necessary and microwave a minute longer. Remove and crumble.

- To dry **wet shoes** fill them with crumpled newspaper and wrap each shoe in newspaper. The paper absorbs the moisture.

- To sharpen a **machine needle,** place a piece of very fine sandpaper under the needle and sew through it as you would a piece of material.

- To make **corned beef** tastier, add a dash of vinegar, a tablespoon of honey and a few cloves while cooking.

- To make **tough meat** tender when boiling, add half a teaspoon of cream of tartar to the water.

- Before making flour into a **batter** for a pudding, add a dessertspoonful of ground rice. This will make the pudding much lighter.

- When frying **fish,** sprinkle a little curry powder into the pan. It prevents the 'fishy' smell and improves flavour and colour.

- A stick of **cinnamon** *or* ½ teaspoon of **cloves** added to the water when stewing apples, peaches, pears or prunes gives them a delightful 'spicy' flavour.

- For a change, try flavouring your **fish** with orange juice instead of lemon.

- Warming **jam** before spreading it on a sponge prevents the jam soaking through.

- To remove **marks** made on a polished table by hot plates, use a mix of linseed oil and turpentine. Gently simmer ½ litre of linseed oil for 10 minutes. Remove it from the stove and add 125*ml* of turpentine. Mix the two ingredients and apply to the burn marks.

- Don't despair if a **meringue** collapses before your very eyes. Top it with some marshmallows then toast it under the grill or in a very hot oven.

- To remove **the smell of smoke** from a room, burn a few drops of vinegar on a hotplate or in a pan.

♦ **Stain removal:**
Cold water removes bloodstains, egg, writing ink. Rinse in lots of cold water and then wash in hot suds.

Warm water removes coffee, tea, ice cream, milk, butter. Then wash in warm suds.

Turpentine removes oil based paint from fabrics.

Methylated spirits removes ballpoint ink, grass, lipstick and mascara.

Glycerine is safe for use on all fabrics and with dyes. It dissolves tannin stains and loosen others.

Acetone, the main ingredient of some nail polish removers, removes paint, varnish and lacquer stains on all fabrics except acetate rayon which it dissolves.

Bleaches remove mildew and, as a last resource, those stains which do not respond to other removers. (Test bleach on a sample piece of material first, in case it takes out the colour or weakens the material.)

A good *window cleaner* is made with 1 cup kerosene, 1 cup methylated spirits and 1 cup of water. Pour these ingredients into a bottle and shake thoroughly. The mixture will keep indefinitely, but always shake well before using. To use, put a few drops on a soft rag and wipe over windows and mirrors. No polishing required.

♦ A cloth dampened with **kerosene** will keep chrome taps shining and highly polished.

♦ To keep **egg yolks** fresh after using just the whites, cover with cold water in a bowl or cup.

♦ To remove **fruit stains** from a handkerchief, soak it in cream of tartar and wash in the usual way.

♦ To clean **porcelain ornaments** and rings use toothpaste.

♦ To stop a **needle** from **breaking** when sewing thick material, rub grease down the seam.

♦ To help **angora wool** go further, knit alternate rows with 2-ply wool.

INDEX OF RECIPES